THE DAEMONS
ROBERT SLOMAN
AND BARRY LETTS

EDITED BY JOHN McELROY

TITAN BOOKS
LONDON

DOCTOR WHO *THE SCRIPTS* : THE DAEMONS
ISBN 1 85286 324 2

Published by
Titan Books
19 Valentine Place
London SE1 8QH

First edition October 1992
10 9 8 7 6 5 4 3 2 1

British Library Cataloguing-in-Publication Data. A catalogue record for
this book is available from the British Library.

By arrangement with BBC Books, a division of BBC Enterprises Ltd

Typeset by Spectrum Typesetting Limited, London.
Printed and bound in Great Britain by Cox and Wyman Ltd, Reading,
Berkshire.

CONTENTS

INTRODUCTION

Ever since its first transmission in the early summer of 1971, *The Dæmons* has rightly been hailed as an example of classic *Doctor Who*. Indeed, a number of fan polls have placed it at the very pinnacle of perfection, naming it the best *Doctor Who* story.

There is great excitement amongst devotees of the series, because after many years of not holding a full, transmittable *colour* copy of this story, the BBC recently went ahead with a fan-inspired experiment to re-add colour to the episodes that previously they held only in black and white. Note, that this is *not* the colourisation process so controversial in the world of the cinema, and so hated by black and white film buffs. Instead, by using a fan-made American copy of the programme in colour (which BBC policy dictates is not up to broadcast standard) and synchronising the colour signal from that to the black and white print that they do hold, a perfect colour copy of the programme, that could be transmitted, would, in theory, be the result.

The experiment worked well. So well, in fact, that at the time of writing the BBC are preparing to transmit the story again, in full colour, for the first time in over twenty years. Although it is largely coincidence that *The Dæmons* was chosen as the first Third Doctor script book, we hope that the script will further increase your enjoyment of what many would say is the ultimate adventure of the good Doctor.

Finally, my grateful thanks to Stephen James Walker for writing the background section to this book at such short notice.

John McElroy, August 1992

BACKGROUND

The Dæmons, written by Barry Letts and Robert Sloman under the pseudonym Guy Leopold, was first transmitted in mid-1971 as the final story of *Doctor Who*'s eighth season - the second featuring Jon Pertwee in the title role. It is regarded by many as the archetypal story of that period and incorporates all the best-remembered elements of an era in which the Doctor, having been exiled to Earth by his own people, the Time Lords, had temporarily ceased his travels through time and space and become unofficial scientific adviser to the British branch of the United Nations Intelligence Taskforce - UNIT for short.

The exile scenario had been conceived some three years earlier by *Doctor Who*'s then producers, Derrick Sherwin and Peter Bryant. Their reasons for wanting to bring the series down to Earth (literally) were twofold: first, they had concluded that their limited budget would no longer stretch to the cost of creating all the special scenery, props and costumes required to represent a succession of alien planets and cultures; secondly, they felt that monsters and other unearthly threats were usually far more frightening and dramatically effective if encountered in familiar, everyday settings.

The UNIT organisation was an integral part of the exile format. It had been created by Sherwin for the season six story *The Invasion* and was reintroduced at the start of season seven, in Pertwee's debut story *Spearhead from Space*, in order to provide a home base for the newly exiled Doctor. With its scientific and military facilities and its remit to deal with 'the odd, the unexplained; anything on Earth, or even beyond', it served as an excellent vehicle to get the Doctor involved in adventures and to help him gain the upper hand at the end of them.

What Sherwin and Bryant had hoped to achieve with this new format (having seen the potential for it in an earlier *Doctor Who* story, *The Web of Fear*) was to recreate the style and atmosphere of the BBC's three hugely successful *Quatermass* science fiction serials of the fifties - and particularly the last of the three, *Quatermass and the Pit*, in which the hero, Professor Bernard Quatermass, is aided by another scientist and his young female assistant and works alongside an army officer in charge of a squad of soldiers. Consequently, season seven saw the Doctor assisted by a young female scientist, Dr Liz Shaw, and working in a somewhat uncomfortable alliance with an army officer, Brigadier Lethbridge-Stewart, and his UNIT troops. The scripts for this season also recalled the gritty, naturalistic quality of the *Quatermass* serials, even borrowing a number of specific plot elements from them, and were rather more adult in tone than most of those commissioned in the earlier *Doctor Who*'s. This was picked up by the stories' directors and reflected in their work.

Season eight retained the basic format established in season seven but saw the series gradually pulling back from this hard, adult type of science fiction and adopting a somewhat lighter, more fantasy-based style - a shift of emphasis attributable largely to the influence of Barry Letts, the new producer who had taken over from Sherwin and Bryant during the making of season seven. Under the guidance of Letts and script editor Terrance Dicks, the series took on a generally cosier and less realistic aspect. So while UNIT continued to be an important element, it bore progressively less resemblance to any real-life military organisation; and while in season seven the Doctor's relationship with the Brigadier had been one of uneasy mutual convenience, during season eight it became one of obvious friendship. The Doctor himself mellowed somewhat as he lost the harder edges of his rather arrogant season seven persona, becoming a debonair and reassuring uncle figure, albeit still a man of action.

These changes coincided with and were reinforced by a gradual toning down of the series' horror content, particularly after the first story of season eight, *Terror of the Autons*, drew considerable criti- cism for being 'too frightening' and even provoked questions in Parliament. In keeping with this renewed emphasis on the series' family viewing status, Letts also expanded the regular cast to create a 'family' of ongoing characters. The Doctor acquired a Time Lord arch-enemy, the Master (played by Roger Delgado), who would appear in every story of season eight; the Brigadier (Nicholas Courtney) gained a second-in-command, Captain Mike Yates (Richard Franklin); Sergeant Benton (John Levene), who had appeared in three previous stories, became a fully fledged regular; Corporal Bell (Fernanda Marlowe) was introduced as another, although more short-lived, member of the UNIT team; and, to succeed Liz Shaw, whose serious-minded and rather straight-laced character was now considered out of place, the Doctor was given a new companion, Jo Grant (Katy Manning), much more akin to the 'screamers' of the series' earlier years.

Jo Grant's introduction was the catalyst which led indirectly to the making of *The Dæmons*. The production team had needed an audition piece when casting the character and for this purpose Barry Letts had written two short scenes, both featuring Captain Yates. The longer of the two involved Yates rescuing Jo from a church. "After he's found her," Letts recalls, "he throws a book onto a strangely carved stone, and the book is immediately torn to shreds by a force he describes as being like an elemental piranha fish; waiting to tear her apart just as effectively. And at the very end Jo turns round and sees the Devil... It was quite an exciting little scene, insofar as Jo had to be terrified and brave and to do a jolly good scream at the end, which is what *Doctor Who* girls have to be good at doing."

Letts had long been interested in tales of black magic, having been particularly thrilled as a boy by Dennis Wheatley's *The Devil Rides Out*, and he was very pleased with the way this audition piece had worked. He subsequently commented to Terrance Dicks that it was a pity they could not have a black magic story in the series itself, to which Dicks replied, "Why not?" Thus it was that Letts decided to expand his short audition piece into a full story:

"I wanted to write *The Dæmons* as a proving vehicle for myself. As producer (and a fairly new one at that), I'd been busy telling writers how I felt *Doctor Who* should be done, but for a long time I'd thought, 'It's all very well telling other people how it should be done, maybe I ought to have a go myself...'"

Letts did not, however, want to write the story entirely on his own, so to help him with the task he contacted a local friend by the name of Robert Sloman. Sloman had never written for television before but was an established playwright, several of whose shows had enjoyed prestigious runs in London's West End. The two men found that they could work very well together, brainstorming ideas between them and then tying them down into a sound dramatic format, and they quickly came up with the basic plot of *The Dæmons*.

The central premise of the story is that of a peaceful, somewhat idealised, rural English village being threatened by an ancient demonic presence - an idea in line with the Sherwin and Bryant philosophy of juxtaposing alien menaces with familiar, everyday settings. This was an approach with which Letts was in wholehearted agreement:

"I firmly believed, and I still do now, that the best *Doctor Who* stories - and the best science fiction stories in general - are those which mix the ordinary and the everyday with the extraordinary and the strange... If you're going from a simple village to the extreme oddity of black magic, then into the realm of science fiction, then finally back again to the village, all the time you have one idea highlighting the others. So I was convinced that *The Dæmons* was a good example of how to write science fiction in general and *Doctor Who* in particular."

Unusually for a UNIT tale, it is not through one of the Brigadier's assignments that the Doctor gets involved in the action of *The Dæmons*. Instead, he whisks Jo off to the curiously named village of Devil's End after seeing a TV broadcast about an archaeological dig at a nearby barrow, the Devil's Hump. When the barrow is opened and powerful forces erupt, Captain Yates and Sergeant Benton have to follow on in the UNIT helicopter. The Brigadier is actually the last of the UNIT regulars to arrive on the scene, his subordinates having to rouse him from his bed with a telephone call. As Barry Letts explains, this all contributed to the development of the characters:

"I wanted to expand on the idea that the members of UNIT were ordinary people with lives of their own and an interaction among themselves. That's why we saw them in civilian dress for once."

Letts had initial doubts as to the feasibility of doing a black magic story. He was concerned that to feature such potentially disturbing subject matter might be inconsistent with the aim of appealing to a tea-time family audience. With this potential pitfall in mind, he and Sloman were careful to ensure that all the phenomena depicted in the story were seen to have a rational explanation, so that the series would not appear to be endorsing the concept of magic.

The opposition between science and magic is indeed one of the strongest themes of the story, with the Doctor at pains to stress that everything which happens in life "must have a scientific explanation" and that magic is "balderdash" and "nonsense." The apparently supernatural forces which the Master, posing as a clergyman, summons up in a cavern below the church in Devil's End are rationalised as a product of "the secret science of the Dæmons."

The story's director, Christopher Barry, also recalls the concern which was felt over its subject matter:

"We did have a minor problem with the black magic angle in that people were a little bit wary about connecting black magic with ecclesiastical premises. There was a certain amount of trepidation about using the old church, and in fact we had to change the name of the underground area where the rites were carried out; we didn't call it the crypt specifically. The idea was that you went down through the vestry door in the church into an underground area, but it was never called the crypt and it was always assumed, if anyone bothered to question it, which I dare say they did at the time, that this was not consecrated ground."

Another arguably rather strange limitation dictated by religious sensibilities was that the script could make no mention of God, in case this was considered blasphemous.

The level of horror in the story continued to cause concern even after its studio recording had been completed, BBC1 Controller Ronald Marsh insisting that the production team edit out a shot of Jo being held down on a sacrificial altar while the Master raises a knife above her. However, despite the care which had been taken, complaints were still received, as Barry Letts explains:

"Afterwards, we had one or two letters complaining that it was wrong to expose children to this kind of evil. I wrote back and said, 'You must understand that this is not real black magic. For example, the spell the Master chants to raise the Dæmon, Azal, is not something like the Lord's Prayer spoken backwards; it is in fact the nursery rhyme *Mary Had a Little Lamb* spoken backwards.'

"This isn't to say there was no research done for the story. I did read quite a few books about black magic to find out the sort of things Satanists did, but only so I could then invent my own rituals and my own words which would sound plausible without actually being the real thing."

The *Quatermass* influence, which had been such an important factor in the conception of the exile format, can still be detected in *The Dæmons*, several aspects of which are highly reminiscent of *Quatermass and the Pit*. In that 1957 serial, an archaeological dig uncovers a long-buried alien spaceship, emanations from which have given the local area a reputation for hauntings and apparitions. Professor Quatermass later discovers that the ship contains creatures who have guided Mankind's development for their own ends and whose gargoyle-like features have entered into folklore as the images of goblins and demons. As the story reaches its climax, a TV news team is caught up in an eruption of psychic energy from the excavation site and the alien menace manifests itself as a huge creature towering over the area - a menace which is ultimately defeated only through an act of supreme self-sacrifice by one of Quatermass's associates. All these plot elements are closely mirrored in *The Dæmons*.

The most notable of the relatively small number of incidental characters in *The Dæmons* is the local white witch, Miss Hawthorne, a delightful eccentric with an indomitable spirit and a crystal ball in her handbag. She is the first to realise the dangers of excavating the Devil's Hump, and she also takes an instant dislike to the Master - alias the Reverend Mr Magister - recognising him for the charlatan that he is.

The Dæmons is an excellent vehicle for the Master, who seems to be very much in his element as, bedecked in flowing scarlet robes, he takes charge of the unholy rites of the local coven, fiercely declaiming the bizarre incantations which will summon Azal to appear before them. Unusually for a major villain, he is introduced quite early on in the first episode. However, as *The Dæmons* concluded a season in which he had appeared in every story, the revelation of his presence would no doubt have come as little surprise to viewers. The closing moments of *The Dæmons* actually bring to an end this regular run of appearances as the Master is finally taken prisoner by UNIT and driven off under armed guard - and to a chorus of jeering from the Devil's End villagers - to await trial for his crimes.

The Doctor's other adversaries on this occasion are the stone gargoyle Bok, brought to life by Azal's power, and the ancient Dæmon himself. Bok is an interesting departure from the norm of the series' monsters. Although essentially an instrument of the Master's will, he also has a mind of his own and is shown to harbour a superstitious fear of magic! Azal, meanwhile, is one of a number of awesomely powerful superbeings featured in this era of *Doctor Who*'s history (others being Kronos in *The Time Monster* and Omega in *The Three Doctors*). His form is that of the popular image of the Devil - complete with horns and cloven hooves - but he is presented as being not so much evil as amoral, treating the human race as a scientific experiment which can be discarded if judged a failure. It is arguably one of the story's few weak points that in the end he is defeated relatively easily, simply self-destructing when faced with the apparent illogicality of Jo's willingness to sacrifice her own life to save the Doctor's. Clearly the writers were drawing a religious parallel here.

Location filming for *The Dæmons* took place over a week-and-a-half in early May 1971 in the picturesque village of Aldbourne in Wiltshire, seven miles north west of Hungerford.

"Aldbourne was a very difficult location to find," notes Christopher Barry. "In fact we had to recruit extra production managers. What I was looking for was a village with a village green, off a main road, and it had to be near enough to a long barrow and to somewhere else, a disused airfield would be ideal, where we could film the chase sequence. We started with ordnance survey maps and reference books which I had because of my interest in archaeology. We ringed practically every long barrow in Britain, visited them and took photographs of them. There were hundreds of long barrows, and in the end we didn't use a long barrow at all, we settled for a couple of bell barrows. We settled for those because there they were, just up a track from Aldbourne.

"Aldbourne had a lovely church, it was a quiet village, it had a village green where we could land a helicopter, it had a pub on the green, the church was on the green and the main road was down the other end of the village so we wouldn't interrupt traffic. It was lovely and ideal. There was Marlborough only a few miles away where we could find hotels to stay in; and the disused airfield at Membury, which is now the site of the Membury service station on the M4, we could use for the chase and for the scenes at the beginning with Bessie."

Location work at this point in the series' history usually followed the standard technique of shooting with a single film camera, each scene being repeated several times from a variety of different angles so that a selection of the resulting footage could later be edited together for use in the finished programme. On *The Dæmons*, however, there was so much film work to be done that Christopher Barry obtained Barry Letts' permission to take three film cameras to the location and use them in a multi-camera set-up, similar to the way electronic cameras are used in a TV studio, thus cutting down considerably the number of takes which had to be done. The cameras were 'crystal locked' together so that all three could be started and stopped simultaneously by remote control.

"We placed under each camera a big sheet of chipboard," explains Christopher Barry, "to act as a sort of platform for the tripods, all of which had wheels so they could change their position slightly, as in the studio. By having the tripods on wheels you could re-align a scene and do decent two-shots without having to stop. The only person it was hell for was the sound man who had three times the amount of worry trying to keep his boom out of shot. All in all it was a compromise, but it did mean effectively we could do three days' work in one."

Even using this technique, it still proved very difficult to complete all the filming in time, owing to the extreme variability of the weather during the location shoot. At one point, there was actually a freak snowstorm!

Studio recording for the story was done in three blocks. Episode one was completed in TC4 (Television Centre Studio 4) on Tuesday May 11th, episodes two and three in TC3 on Wednesday May 19th and episodes five and six in TC3 on Wednesday May 26th.

When *The Dæmons* was transmitted it received average ratings of 8.34 million viewers per episode and an average position of twenty-fifth on the weekly TV chart, both very respectable figures. An edited compilation repeat was screened later the same year, on 28th December, and this received an even higher rating of 10.53 million viewers, although it reached only thirty-eighth position on the TV chart as it was in competition with many blockbuster Christmas programmes. The story remains a firm favourite both with fans and with those who contributed to it, all the regular cast members citing it as one of the best and most enjoyable they worked on.

"I've heard it said that this era of the programme was a very happy one," says Christopher Barry, "and I think I would agree with that. Jon Pertwee had an aura about him which spread jollity, as he was a comedian first and foremost. I don't remember coming in and thinking 'This is the nicest job I've ever done because they're all so friendly,' or anything like that. I was just accepted and welcomed mutually."

However, Barry cautions against looking back at the production with rose-tinted glasses, pointing out that not everything was sweetness and light:

"I actually had a very bitter experience at the time. We were filming at Aldbourne and because we'd had this wretched snowstorm we were running over and had to work on the weekend in order to catch up. I wanted to work on the Sunday and have the Saturday off so that I could go to my sister's wedding. However, a certain Mr Who had a cabaret engagement down in Portsmouth that night which he intended to keep as it was worth several hundred pounds to him, and he refused to do it my way. So I couldn't go to the wedding. I sent a telegram saying 'Best wishes, Doctor Who has prevented me from coming,' which was read out by the best man!"

Despite having mixed feelings about the production, Christopher

Barry was well pleased with the finished result. Barry Letts was also happy with the way the story turned out:

"I think that what came out of *The Dæmons* was a renewed faith in my practice of asking writers to think not so much as scriptwriters but more as playwrights. Scriptwriters, particularly for series, very often sit down and write a scene which has to go from A to B, and what they write is a perfectly good sequence which does go from A to B. But a playwright, writing the same scene, won't always write straight down the middle; sometimes he'll try to come into it from the side. With *The Dæmons*, very often what the characters were talking about wasn't necessarily strictly to do with the central plot, it was more to do with relationships, even though ultimately those relationships would have a bearing on the central theme.

"I don't think I succeeded completely - obviously as it was the first time I'd tried it. But I did want to see if I could do what I was telling everybody else to do. The village was a cliché with many of the characters instantly recognisable. It wasn't the first time someone had written about an English village with black magic going on, and it certainly won't be the last. But what I wanted to do was to take that cliché and make it not a cliché, and to fill it with people one could be interested in. I think we did pretty well."

Stephen James Walker, July 1992

With acknowledgements to Barry Letts, Robert Sloman, Christopher Barry, Jeremy Bentham and David J. Howe.

CAST

The Doctor	Jon Pertwee
Jo Grant	Katy Manning
Brigadier Lethbridge-Stewart	Nicholas Courtney
The Master	Roger Delgado
Captain Mike Yates	Richard Franklin
Sergeant Benton	John Levene
Professor Gilbert Horner	Robin Wentworth (Episodes 1,2)
Miss Olive Hawthorne	Damaris Hayman
Bok	Stanley Mason (Episodes 2-5)
Azal	Stephen Thorne (Episodes 4,5)
Bert the landlord	Don McKillop
Squire Winstanley	Rollo Gamble (Episodes 1-3)
Tom Girton	Jon Croft (Episodes 1-3)
Garvin	John Joyce (Episodes 1,2)
Alastair Fergus	David Simeon (Episode 1)
Harry	James Snell (Episodes 1,2)
Doctor Reeves	Eric Hillyard (Episodes 2,3)
Sergeant Osgood	Alec Linstead (Episodes 3-5)
Thorpe	John Owens (Episodes 3-5)
Morris dancer (stunt)	Peter Diamond (Episode 4)
Jones	Matthew Corbett (Episode 5)
PC Groom	Christopher Wray (Episodes 1,2)
RAF pilot (voice)	Christopher Barry (Episode 3)
Morris dancers	The Headington Quarry Men (Episode 4)

Extras

Episode 1 only: John Holmes, Lily Harrold

Episodes 1 and 2: Ronald Mayer, Jimmy Mac, Michael Earl, Patrick Milner, Richard Lawrence, Roy Pearce, Robin Squire, Alan Lenoire, Sonnie Willis, Roy Oliver Bruce Humble, Simon Malloy

Episodes 1-3: Charles Finch

Episodes 1 and 3: Mo Race

Episodes 1, 2, 4 and 5: John Tatham, David J. Graham, Vic Taylor

Episode 2 only: Leslie Bates, Stephen Ismay, Ron Tingley, Anthony Case, Gerald Taylor

Episode 3 only: Pamela Deveraux, John Crane, J. W. Phillips, R. Dixon, Paul Stone, George Mackie, Gladys Bacon, Renne Roberts, Keith Ashley, Bill Lodge, Bill Gosling, Walter Goodman, Ian Elliott, Peter Diamond

Episodes 3 and 4: Ron Taylor

Episodes 3 and 5: Jim Davidson, Andrew Butcher, Terry Denton, Michael Moore, Bill Burridge, Ernest Blythe, Lawrence Archer, Rex Rashley, Charles Shaw Hesketh, Geoff Witherick, John Scott Martin

Episode 4 only: Jack Silk, Lesley Matcham

Episodes 4 and 5: Pat Gorman, Les Osman, Myrtle Osman, Jean Scaife, Maria Burns, Kathy Ryan, Lyn Matcham

Episode 5 only: Frank Bennett, Ray James, Daryl Grove, Terry Rolph, Ray Taylor, Helge Borgen, Gary Edwards, Monica Kidd, Jane Woods, Beryl Houghton, Bob James, Clive Wentzal, Roger Marcham, Monty Yerger, Dave Martin, S. Ford, S. Madden, Jerry Melbourne, Robin Ford

TECHNICAL DETAILS

Story code: JJJ

Story title: The Dæmons

Working title: The Demons

Authors: Barry Letts and Robert Sloman (writing under the pseudonym Guy Leopold)

Number of episodes: 5

Studio recording dates: 11th May 1971

19th May 1971

26th May 1971

Episode One

Duration...................................... 25'0"

First transmitted .... 22nd May 1971, at 18:16:50

Episode Two

Duration...................................... 24'20"

First transmitted .... 29th May 1971, at 18:10:31

Episode Three

Duration...................................... 24'27"

First transmitted .... 5th June 1971, at 18:11:20

Episode Four

Duration...................................... 24'25"

First transmitted .... 12th June 1971, at 18:11:20

Episode Five

Duration...................................... 24'04"

First transmitted .... 19th June 1971, at 18:10:40

(Edited version of complete story transmitted 28th December 1971)

PRODUCTION CREDITS

Producer	Barry Letts
Script editor	Terrance Dicks
Director	Christopher Barry
Designer	Roger Ford
Production assistant	Peter Grimwade
Assistant floor manager	Sue Hedden
Studio sound	Ralph Walton
Studio lighting	Tony Millier
Film cameraman	Fred Hamilton
Film camera operators	David South
	Pat Turley
	Paul Wheeler
Film sound	Dick Manton
Film editor	Chris Wimble
Visual effects	Peter Day
Costumes	Barbara Lane
Make-up	Jan Harrison
Fight arranger	Peter Diamond
Incidental music	Dudley Simpson
Special sound	Brian Hodgson
Theme music	Ron Grainer
	BBC Radiophonic Workshop
Title sequence	Bernard Lodge

EPISODE ONE

1. A Village Street (Night).

(Torrential rain batters the village of Devil's End. Thunder crashes and lightning lights up the village and the local church. In the churchyard, something is moving secretly about, snuffling through the foliage. The only light to be seen comes from the village pub. We see the sign 'The Cloven Hoof', which sways violently in the gale-force winds. A man comes out of the pub. He has a dog with him, on a lead, and with his free hand he tries to keep his hat from blowing away. As they walk past the churchyard, the dog growls, pulls away from the man, and then dashes through the church gate, barking furiously. The dog's barking turns into a yelp, then silence. From nearby comes a high-pitched chattering noise.)

2. A Churchyard.

(The man, slightly the worse for drink, staggers into the churchyard looking for his dog. The chattering sound comes again. He looks up - and opens his mouth to scream in terror at what he sees. The scream dies in his throat.)

3. A VILLAGE STREET (DAY).

(MISS HAWTHORNE, *a somewhat eccentrically dressed lady in her fifties, is pestering* DOCTOR REEVES *as he makes his way to his car.*)

HAWTHORNE: He died of fright, Doctor.

REEVES: My dear Miss Hawthorne...

HAWTHORNE: I don't care what you say. The man died of fright!

REEVES: My dear Miss Hawthorne, the medical diagnosis was quite clear. He died of a heart attack.

HAWTHORNE: But his face...!

REEVES: Slight protrusion of the eyeballs; rictus drawing of the lips back over the teeth. Common enough in heart failure.

HAWTHORNE: The signs are there for all to see. I cast the runes only this morning.

REEVES: You'll have to excuse me. I have my rounds to do.

HAWTHORNE: If Professor Horner opens up that barrow, he will bring disaster on us all...

(REEVES *drives away.* MISS HAWTHORNE *calls after him, with intense conviction in her voice.*)

This is just the beginning!

4. EXTERIOR THE BARROW.

(*The barrow is clearly the scene of an archaeological dig. BBC outside broadcast cameras are present and* HARRY *and the other assistants bustle around.* ALISTAIR FERGUS, *the presenter of the TV programme, is in the middle of all the activity.)*

HARRY (*oov*):	A bit more, David.
FERGUS:	Professor Horner!
HARRY (*oov*):	That's it.
FERGUS:	Oh, where's he got to for Pete's sake? Harry!

(HARRY, FERGUS's *personal assistant, comes bustling up.)*

HARRY:	Hello Alistair - what's up?
FERGUS:	Where's Professor Horner?
HARRY:	Probably in make-up... unless he's had second thoughts and scarpered!
FERGUS:	What!
HARRY:	Well, you know the local chat. Death and disaster if he opens the barrow.
FERGUS:	Well, there'll be a disaster if he doesn't get a shift on.
HARRY:	Okay, okay, I'll chase him up.

(HARRY *bustles off.* FERGUS *shakes his head at the chaos all around him.)*

5. *THE UNIT WORKSHOP.*

(THE DOCTOR *is fiddling with something in Bessie, his car's innards.* JO GRANT *is standing nearby handing various spanners, etc, to him as he asks for them.)*

JO:	But it really *is* the dawning of the age of Aquarius.

THE DOCTOR: So?

JO: Well, that means the occult. Well you know, the supernatural and all that magic bit.

THE DOCTOR: You know really, Jo... I'm obviously wasting my time trying to turn you into a scientist.

JO: Well how do you know there's nothing in it?

THE DOCTOR: How? Well I just know, that's all. Everything that happens in life must have a scientific explanation... if you know where to look for it that is. Excuse me.

> *(Whilst* THE DOCTOR *has been talking he has closed Bessie's bonnet and walked over to a bench, where he picks something up and puts it in one of his pockets.)*

JO: Yes, but... but suppose something was to happen and nobody knew the explanation - well, nobody in the world... in the universe. Well that would be magic, wouldn't it?

THE DOCTOR: You know Jo, for a reasonably intelligent young lady, you do have the most absurd ideas!

> *(As they continue talking, Bessie's motor starts running and she slowly drives out of the workshop and turns in a circle outside, before heading back towards the workshop.* JO *sees this happening and, as* THE DOCTOR *continues talking, her eyes nearly pop out of her head.)*

JO: Doctor. Look!

> *(Bessie pulls up alongside them.)*

THE DOCTOR: Bessie! How dare you go gallivanting around like that?

(Bessie beeps her horn.)

Are you sorry?

(Bessie beeps her horn twice. JO'*s eyes practically pop out.)*

Very well, I forgive you. Now go back to your parking place before I change my mind.

(Bessie does as she is told, just as MIKE YATES *walks into the room.)*

YATES: I know there's a good explanation for all this, but I just can't think of it for the moment.

THE DOCTOR: Would you believe magic?

YATES: Magic?

THE DOCTOR: Mm.

YATES: No.

THE DOCTOR: Well, Jo would.

JO: That's not fair.

THE DOCTOR: Well you explain it then.

JO: Oh, I don't know. I suppose you did it.

THE DOCTOR: Naturally. Or should I say scientifically. Solenoids and a servo-mechanism in Bessie, and a radio control unit here.

(He produces a small box from his pocket.)

You see how easy it is to be a magician?

JO: How infuriating can you get? Well it doesn't prove anything.

THE DOCTOR: Would you like me to show you some more then?

JO: No thanks. I've had enough of your knavish tricks. Anyway, I want to see that TV programme. Mike, would you give me a lift?

YATES: Sure.

JO: Thanks.

YATES: You coming, Doctor?

THE DOCTOR: Coming where?

YATES: Well, to see that programme.

THE DOCTOR: Not you too, Captain Yates?

YATES: Wouldn't miss it for worlds. Very exciting. Forecasts of doom and disaster if anyone disturbs the burial chamber.

THE DOCTOR: Captain Yates, you astound me.

YATES: Well, you never know. Devil's End has a funny reputation.

THE DOCTOR: What did you say?

YATES: Devil's End. The village near the dig.

THE DOCTOR: Devil's End... Devil's End...

YATES: Doctor... are you all right?

THE DOCTOR: Yes, yes I'm fine... fine.

    (It obviously rings a very large and very disturbing bell. THE DOCTOR *suddenly 'comes to', grabs his jacket and strides out of the workshop towards Bessie.)*

YATES: Now where are you going?

THE DOCTOR: To see that TV programme of course!

6. THE CAVERN.

(The cavern is a mixture of crypt and cave. Alcoves in the walls contain tableaux of hooded figures up to no good and in a niche a gargoyle figure crouches. ALISTAIR FERGUS *is busy addressing the camera, pausing dramatically in the middle of his sentences.)*

FERGUS: Devil's End... the very name sends a shiver up the spine. The witches of Devil's End... the famous curse... the notorious cavern underneath the church where the third Lord Aldbourne played at his eighteenth century parody of black magic. Devil's End is part of the... dark mythology of our childhood days. And now for the first time the... cameras of the BBC have been allowed inside the cavern itself... In this cavern pagan man performed his unspeakable rites; in this cavern the witches of the seventeenth century hid from the fires of Matthew Hopkins, witch-hunter extraordinary; in this cavern... but I could go on all day. There is... something strange about Devil's End. Is Professor Horner being as... foolish as his critics would suggest? I must admit, standing here in this... unquiet place... I'm beginning to wonder myself...

7. EXTERIOR THE BARROW (SOME TIME LATER).

HARRY: Quiet please!

FERGUS: While I was recording that earlier this afternoon, the archaeological dig was proceeding apace. Professor Horner and his team have cut their way into the Devil's Hump, as this barrow is called by the locals, as if it were a giant pie. But now the question is, can Professor Horner pull out his plum?

(He chuckles, amused at his own witticism. Nearby, stands PROFESSOR HORNER, *not nearly as amused.)*

HORNER: Get on with it, man.

FERGUS: Or will the Professor be proved disastrously wrong?

8. UNIT HQ DUTY ROOM.

*(*SERGEANT BENTON *is busy watching the TV programme and* FERGUS'S *voice continues in the background.)*

FERGUS (*oov*): For some 200 years the controversy has raged. What is the Devil's Hump? Now we are not the first to try to find out. But from 1793 when Sir Percival Flint's miners ran back to Cornwall, leaving him for dead, to the... famous Cambridge University fiasco of 1939...

*(*THE DOCTOR, JO *and* CAPTAIN YATES *come into the room.)*

JO: Has it started yet?

BENTON: Sssh!

FERGUS (*oov*): ... the Devil's Hump has remained an enigma.

THE DOCTOR: Let's see what he has to say.

(They all watch.)

FERGUS (*oov*): But tonight, the enigma will be solved.

9. *EXTERIOR THE BARROW.*

FERGUS (*oov*): Tonight at midnight, the witching hour, viewers of BBC 3 will have the privilege of being present when Professor Gilbert Horner, the noted archaeologist...

HORNER: Got around to me at last, have you?

(PROFESSOR HORNER *strides into shot, beckoning the cameraman to follow as he enters the barrow.*)

And about time too!

FERGUS: Not yet Professor, not yet!

(FERGUS *whispers angrily to* PROFESSOR HORNER, *who ignores him.*)

HORNER: Hey, bring that camera over here, will you. Come on.

(FERGUS, *clearly embarrased, is forced to follow the Professor and beckons the cameraman after him.*)

10. *INTERIOR THE BARROW.*

(PROFESSOR HORNER *moves through the cavern followed by* FERGUS *and the cameraman.*)

HORNER: There. That's the spot. Six inches behind there lies the greatest archaeological find this country has known since Sutton Hoo.

FERGUS: Would you like to explain that reference, Professor?

HORNER: No. And at midnight tonight...

FERGUS: Sutton Hoo, of course...

HORNER:	Never mind about Sutton Hoo. This is what your precious viewers are interested in. The Devil's Hump and what's inside it. Right?
FERGUS:	And what is inside it?
HORNER:	Treasure, that's what. The tomb of a great warrior chieftain. Bronze Age. 800 BC.
FERGUS:	You're very precise.
HORNER:	No need to take my word for it. See for yourself. Midnight.
FERGUS:	Ah yes. Now then, why midnight? And why tonight?
HORNER:	Well it's obvious. April 30th is Beltane, isn't it?
FERGUS:	Beltane?
HORNER:	You know, you ought to have done your homework before you came on this dig.
FERGUS:	For the viewers, Professor.
HORNER:	April 30th, Beltane. Greatest occult festival of the year, bar Hallowe'en.

11. UNIT HQ DUTY ROOM.

(The television can still be heard in the background.)

FERGUS (*oov*):	Well, frankly, I'm not much wiser.
THE DOCTOR:	Beltane. Of course!
HORNER (*oov*):	You've heard the tales about this place. The ghosts, the witches, the curse... the famous curse.
FERGUS (*oov*):	You don't believe that?

HORNER (*oov*):	Do you?
FERGUS (*oov*):	Well then... er... why...?
HORNER (*oov*):	My new book comes out tomorrow.
FERGUS (*oov*):	Ah then, it's what one might call a publicity gimmick?

(FERGUS *pauses triumphantly, not reckoning on the dour Yorkshireman's response.*)

HORNER (*oov*):	Top of the class, lad.
FERGUS (*oov*):	And you're not concerned about being...
THE DOCTOR:	There's something dreadfully wrong here.
JO:	Hey, you really mean that, don't you?
YATES:	What could be wrong?
THE DOCTOR:	I don't know... Aquarius... The Devil's Hump... Beltane... Come on, think. Think!
BENTON:	Doctor, look... there's something going on.

(*They all look towards the TV set, where a struggle is going on.* MISS HAWTHORNE *is shaking off* HARRY, *who is trying to keep her back from the TV cameras.*)

12. EXTERIOR THE BARROW.

HARRY:	Now, come on luv, be a good girl, and...
HAWTHORNE:	Let me go!

(MISS HAWTHORNE *pushes* HARRY *aside and marches towards* FERGUS *and* PROFESSOR HORNER.)

I have come here to protest and protest I shall.

FERGUS:	Okay, Harry.

(FERGUS *turns back towards the camera.*)

FERGUS: This is Miss Hawthorne, a prominent local resident who is very much opposed to Professor Horner's dig. Professor Horner, I believe you two have already met.

HORNER: I'll say. The daft woman's been pestering me for weeks.

HAWTHORNE: I've been trying to make you see reason...

FERGUS: Miss Hawthorne, why are you so opposed to this dig?

HAWTHORNE: Because this man is tampering with forces he does not understand.

HORNER: Oh come on now.

HAWTHORNE: You will bring destruction upon yourself and upon the whole area if you persist.

HORNER: Rubbish!

HAWTHORNE: Death and disaster await you. Believe me, I know.

FERGUS: But that's just it. Why should we believe you and how do you know?

HAWTHORNE: I am a witch.

HORNER: You see? I told you she was daft!

FERGUS: Miss Hawthorne, you don't really mean...

HAWTHORNE: I tell you, I'm a witch. White, of course. And that is why you should listen to me, I know.

FERGUS: Well, thank you very much Miss Hawthorne for a most interesting...

HAWTHORNE: I have cast the runes; I have consulted the Talisman of Mercury; it is written in the stars: When Beltane is come, tread softly, for lo, the Prince himself is nigh. And tonight is Beltane.

HORNER: You see? Mad as a hatter!

FERGUS: The Prince?

HAWTHORNE: The Prince of Evil; the Dark One; the Horned Beast.

13. UNIT HQ DUTY ROOM.

THE DOCTOR: Come on, Jo.

(THE DOCTOR *leaps into action and heads for the door.*)

JO: Where to?

THE DOCTOR: Devil's End, of course. That woman was perfectly right. We've got to stop that lunatic before it's too late.

(JO *follows, leaving* YATES *and* BENTON *bewildered.*)

14. EXTERIOR THE BARROW.

FERGUS (*oov*): Miss Hawthorne. Professor Horner. Thank you.

(*As he speaks the camera zooms in on him, blocking out the image of* MISS HAWTHORNE, *who is still noisily objecting.*)

So there we are. it seems that time is running out in more ways than one. What is going to happen at midnight? Why not tune in to BBC 3 at 11.45 tonight and find out? Until then, from me it's goodbye now. Alistair Fergus, The Passing Parade. Devil's End.

15. THE CLOVEN HOOF PUB.

(The locals are all watching television, including WINSTANLEY, *the local squire,* TOM GIRTON *and* BERT, *the landlord of the pub.)*

WINSTANLEY: Good for Miss Hawthorne. She kept her end up jolly well.

BERT: Woman's round the twist if you ask me. Always has been.

GIRTON: You're right, Bert. Should have been put away years ago.

WINSTANLEY: Well, I'm not so sure that she hasn't got a point. Broadly speaking, you know.

GIRTON: What, all that stuff about death and disaster? You're not telling me you believe it, Mr Winstanley?

WINSTANLEY: Well, no. But there have been a lot of queer goings on the last few weeks. Strange, sudden noises and er... gusts of wind and poor old Jim dropping down in the churchyard.

BERT: Yeah, Frank was telling me his cows have gone dry - and my wife's hens have stopped laying.

WINSTANLEY: And all since they started digging up there on Devil's Hump.

BERT: Could just be a coincidence.

GIRTON: And we've had a spell of bad weather. Always upsets things that does.

WINSTANLEY: Yes, but just suppose she's right, eh? How about that, Bert?

BERT: Well, I'll tell you. If the Old 'un does come along here tonight, he can have my best room. My bread and butter, he is.

(They all laugh.)

16. THE VILLAGE GREEN.

(POLICE CONSTABLE GROOM *comes out of his house to his bike. He sees* MISS HAWTHORNE *passing by.*)

PC GROOM: Good evening, Miss Hawthorne. Saw you on the television just now. Very good, I thought you were.

HAWTHORNE: They chopped me! Cut me off! But don't you worry, constable. I'll get my chance later tonight. You'll see!

(MISS HAWTHORNE *marches off, but as she nears the churchyard, a sudden, fierce wind springs up without warning, almost knocking her over. At the same time,* PC GROOM *hears a shrill whistling which seems to pierce his skull. He staggers for a moment and then becomes calm, as if in a trance. Just down the road,* MISS HAWTHORNE *recovers herself. She lifts her arms high, her hair and shawl billowing in the wind, and starts to chant.*)

Avaunt, all ye elementals. Avaunt all ye powers of adversity. Be still and return to thy resting. Be at peace in thy sleeping.

(During this, PC GROOM, *still moving as if in a trance, picks up a large stone. He moves up behind* MISS HAWTHORNE *and is clearly about to*

hit her head from behind with the stone, but as he raises it above his head, the exorcism appears to succeed. The wind drops, and as it does POLICE CONSTABLE GROOM *lowers his arms. As whatever power that had overtaken him drops, he comes out of his trance and gazes mystified at the stone that he is still holding.* MISS HAWTHORNE *turns and notices his face.)*

Mr Groom... Mr Groom. Are you all right?

PC GROOM: Yes... I think so. I just felt a bit faint for a moment.

*(*MISS HAWTHORNE *nods sagely.)*

HAWTHORNE: I'm not at all surprised. Not at all. It'll pass, Mr Groom, it'll pass.

PC GROOM: I'm feeling a lot better now already. Thank you.

HAWTHORNE: We must be on our guard. All of us.

(She turns and continues down the road. PC GROOM *looks at the stone in his hand and shakes his head in bewilderment.)*

17. A COUNTRY ROAD (EVENING).

*(*THE DOCTOR *and* JO *are racing along in Bessie. Just ahead of them is a crossroads, with a sign-post, one arm of which points to Devil's End. Suddenly the strange wind springs up and the signpost turns so that all its arms point in the wrong direction. As* THE DOCTOR *passes it he sees the sign to Devil's End and follows it.)*

18. THE CHURCHYARD.

(MISS HAWTHORNE *is walking towards the rectory, when* GARVIN, *the verger, steps out, blocking her path.*)

HAWTHORNE: Oh!

GARVIN: What do you want?

HAWTHORNE: How dare you jump out at me like that? Out of my way please.

GARVIN: What do you want?

HAWTHORNE: Well, if you must know, I wish to contact the vicar.

GARVIN: Mr Magister's not in at the moment.

HAWTHORNE: Not him! I mean the real vicar.

GARVIN: What would you call Mr Magister then?

HAWTHORNE: I mean Canon Smallwood, our old vicar. The one who left in such mysterious circumstances.

GARVIN: Nothing mysterious about it. Taken ill and had to leave.

HAWTHORNE: Suddenly, in the middle of the night? Without so much as a goodbye to anyone in the village?

GARVIN: I've got no time to listen to your nonsense. I've got my work to do.

(*Despite this he does not move, and continues to bar* MISS HAWTHORNE'*s way.*)

HAWTHORNE: Very well then, I'll see the other gentleman. I cannot say that I like him, but he at least is a man of the cloth.

GARVIN: I told you, didn't I. He's not in.

HAWTHORNE: Well, I intend to find that out for myself. Let me pass, please.

GARVIN: You're wasting your time.

HAWTHORNE: If you don't stand out of my way Garvin, I shall be forced to use violence.

> (*The vicar has come up behind them, unnoticed.* MISS HAWTHORNE *turns around and looks straight into the face of...* THE MASTER!)

THE MASTER: Dear me, I hope that violence will not be necessary. Good evening Miss Hawthorne. What can I do for you?

> *19. UNIT HQ DUTY ROOM.*
>
> (CAPTAIN YATES *gets a drink from a vending machine.* SERGEANT BENTON *puts the phone down in disgust.*)

BENTON: Well, that's made a mess of my evening.

> (THE BRIGADIER *comes in from his office. He is wearing full evening dress.* BENTON *rises to attention.*)

BRIGADIER: Everything in order, Yates?

YATES: Yes, sir. No problems.

BRIGADIER: Right then ... Right then, I'm off. You know where to reach me if anything crops up.

YATES: Yes sir. Have a good evening, sir.

> (YATES *glances knowingly at* BENTON. THE BRIGADIER *gives* YATES *a look, as he detects a note of sarcasm in his voice, but decides to let it pass.*)

BRIGADIER: Thank you, Captain Yates. Good night.

YATES: Night, sir.

BENTON: Good night, sir.

               (THE BRIGADIER *exits.*)

               All right for some, isn't it sir? And we're stuck here
               with the television and a plate of corned beef sand-
               wiches.

               20. *THE CHURCHYARD.*

               (GARVIN *watches sullenly while* MISS HAWTHORNE
               pleads with THE MASTER.)

HAWTHORNE: I beg you to help me, Mr Magister. Help me to stop
               that foolhardy man.

THE MASTER: You mean the Professor? But surely...

HAWTHORNE: He must not enter the tomb. Tonight of all nights.

THE MASTER: But why ever not?

HAWTHORNE: Beltane. The forces of evil are abroad tonight.

THE MASTER: Really, Miss Hawthorne. As a rational man I only...

HAWTHORNE: We're all in mortal peril, vicar. Have you no concern
               for the souls in your care?

THE MASTER: The soul as such is a very dated concept. Viewing
               the matter existentially...

HAWTHORNE: Existentially? Oh, you are a blockhead, sir!

               (*She turns to go.*)

THE MASTER: Miss Hawthorne. One moment.

               (MISS HAWTHORNE *turns back.*)

You are very distressed, I can see that.

(As he is speaking, he moves closer to MISS HAWTHORNE, *takes off the glasses he has been wearing and stares into her eyes.)*

You know you really are worrying unduly. There's nothing to worry you. You must believe me. You must believe me.

(For a moment it looks as if THE MASTER *is succeeding in hypnotising her and she starts to go into a trance.)*

HAWTHORNE: Must believe you...

(Then suddenly she jerks herself free of his influence.)

Why should I believe you? A rationalist, existentialist priest, indeed!

*(*THE MASTER *is livid, not accustomed to mere humans being able to resist him.)*

THE MASTER: Listen to me!

HAWTHORNE: You are a fool, sir. If you won't help me, I must find someone who will.

(As she speaks she holds the cross she is wearing around her neck out in front of her. She turns and sweeps away. THE MASTER *is furious. He snaps his fingers at* GARVIN, *who follows* MISS HAWTHORNE.)*

21. A COUNTRY LANE (NIGHT).

(Bessie comes round a corner and stops.)

THE DOCTOR: It's no good, we're hopelessly lost.

(JO *peers at the map she is holding with a torch.*)

JO: I can't understand it. We followed the signposts all right.

THE DOCTOR: If we had we'd have been there by now. You must have missed one.

JO: I did not!

(THE DOCTOR *takes the map from* JO *and turns it the other way up.*)

THE DOCTOR: If you looked at the map the right way up we might eventually get there. Now which way is it?

JO: Mm.... that way.

(*She points in one direction.*)

THE DOCTOR: Thank you very much.

22. *EXTERIOR THE BARROW.*

(ALISTAIR FERGUS *is busy, pacing up and down, his nerves getting the better of him.*)

HARRY: You all right, Alistair?

FERGUS: Of course I am all right! Why shouldn't I be, for Pete's sake? Of all the stupid questions.

HARRY: Well, I only asked. There's no need to make a production number out of it.

FERGUS: I'm sorry, Harry. I'm just a bit on edge. It'll be all right.

(HARRY *moves over to* PROFESSOR HORNER.)

HARRY: Everything okay, Professor? Won't be long now.

HORNER:	Any sign of that fool woman?
HARRY:	Ha. Not so far.
HORNER:	Well, keep her away from me. I tell you lad, I'll do her a mischief.
HARRY:	I'll do my best. Now, you've got everything straight? We start with an intro from Alistair, then I'll give you a cue to launch into your spiel.
HORNER:	Spiel?
HARRY:	The chat bit. Momentous occasion and all that.
HORNER:	Oh, aye.
HARRY:	Tom says if you could break into the burial chamber as the church clock strikes the first stroke of midnight, that would be absolutely super.
HORNER:	Right oh, lad. I'll do my best to be absolutely super. Super!

(HARRY *starts to leave, but then turns back.*)

HARRY:	Professor... suppose something does happen?
HORNER:	Like?
HARRY:	Personal appearance of 'you-know-who'.
HORNER:	Well use your initiative, lad. Get your chatty friend over there to interview him!
HARRY:	Of course. Why didn't I think of that?

23. UNIT HQ DUTY ROOM.

(SERGEANT BENTON *is busy, watching a rugby match on the television.* CAPTAIN YATES *comes in.*)

YATES:	Anything happened yet?

BENTON: No sir, not a thing.

YATES: Isn't it about time for the dig?

BENTON: Just about.

(He nods towards the television.)

This is the highlights from the game... Twickenham.

YATES: Better turn over then.

(BENTON is still wrapped up in the game and exclaims indignantly at some injustice on the rugby field.)

BENTON: Hey! Did you see that?

YATES: Quite right too.

BENTON: You're as bad as the ref, you are sir. Oh, no!

YATES: That'll learn him.

(YATES too starts to get involved and they settle down to watch the match.)

24. THE CLOVEN HOOF PUB.

(In spite of the late hour, the pub is still full of people. WINSTANLEY and GIRTON are present. THE DOCTOR and JO enter.)

BERT: Come along now friends, drink up. Sorry sir, well past time.

THE DOCTOR: That's quite all right, we don't want a drink. Just the directions to the Devil's Hump.

JO: Where the dig is.

BERT:	Ah, you're going up there are you? It's all on telly, you know.
THE DOCTOR:	Yes, yes I know, but would you please tell us the way. This is very urgent.
BERT:	Always in a such hurry, you townsfolk. All be the same in a hundred years time, sir.
THE DOCTOR:	I can assure you sir, it will be no such thing.
WINSTANLEY:	You one of those television chaps then?
THE DOCTOR:	I am no sort of chap, sir.
WINSTANLEY:	Forgive me, but I thought well... the costume... the wig...
THE DOCTOR:	Wig!

(JO *sees that* THE DOCTOR *is about to explode.*)

JO:	Now, Doctor...
GIRTON:	What do you want to go up the hump for anyway?
THE DOCTOR:	Now look, there's no time for all these unnecessary questions.
BERT:	All the time in the world, sir.
THE DOCTOR:	I want to go up to the Devil's Hump because I want to stop that lunatic professor of yours from bringing devastation upon you all.

(*There is a groan of disbelief.*)

GIRTON:	Oh, one of Miss Hawthorne's brigade.
THE DOCTOR:	Is nobody here capable of answering a perfectly simply enquiry? What's the matter with you all?
WINSTANLEY:	You're making all the fuss, old man.

THE DOCTOR: Fuss! I have never heard such balderdash...

JO: Doctor!

(She turns sweetly to WINSTANLEY.*)*

Look, could you please tell us the way?

WINSTANLEY: Yes, certainly. Straight past the green outside, fork left, straight up the rise, and you can't miss it.

THE DOCTOR: Excellent. Thank you very much.

JO: Thank you. Goodbye.

(They rush out.)

WINSTANLEY: What an extraordinary fellow.

25. THE VESTRY.

*(*THE MASTER *is there, with* GARVIN *nearby.* GIRTON *has just arrived from the pub.)*

GIRTON: White hair he had, and a sort of cloak...

THE MASTER: Did he by any chance call himself 'the Doctor'?

GIRTON: That's right. That's what the girl called him. How did you know that?

THE MASTER: It's of no importance.

(He motions GARVIN *to leave.)*

Well Girton, you have done very well. But why aren't you ready?

GIRTON: Well, I thought I should tell you. Saying he was going to stop the dig.

THE MASTER: You'd better hurry and change. We start the ceremony in a few minutes.

(As GIRTON *leaves,* THE MASTER *gets out a magnifi-
cent scarlet robe, marked with cabbalistic signs.)*

26. THE CAVERN.

*(*THE MASTER *enters the cavern. He is now wearing the robe. A number of figures, robed in black,
are setting up a heavy stone below the high altar.
This is the stone of sacrifice.* THE MASTER *looks
over at a gargoyle, perched in an alcove.)*

27. EXTERIOR THE BARROW.

*(The various crew members of the television unit
are chattering away.* ALISTAIR FERGUS, *a charming
smile glazed onto his face, stands waiting for his
cue.)*

HARRY: Quiet please. Lots of lovely hush. Quiet!

(There is a moment of dead silence.)

Stand by. On the studio announcement now. Good
luck from Tom...

(He raises his hand. There is a pause. He drops it.
FERGUS *slides smoothly into his introduction.)*

FERGUS: Welcome back, viewers. And here, at the Devil's
Hump, the excitement is intense. The stage is set.
What shall we see when the curtain rises?

28. *A COUNTRY LANE.*

(THE DOCTOR *and* JO *are speeding furiously along in Bessie.)*

29. *THE CAVERN.*

(A coven of twelve figures, including GIRTON *and* GARVIN, *moan an unintelligible chant.* THE MASTER *throws some incense into the thurible and there is a puff of smoke.)*

THE MASTER: As my will, so mote it be.

COVEN: Nema.

(THE MASTER *sprinkles water over the stone of sacrifice, on which are seven black candles, a chalice and thurible covered with runic signs, and a black cloth.)*

THE MASTER: Harken to my voice, O Dark One; ancient and awful; supreme in artifice; bearer of power; I conjure thee! Be present here at my command and truly do my will. Eva, Evara, Egabala! Gad, Gadoal, Galdina!

COVEN: Io Evohe!

THE MASTER: As my will, so mote it be.

(THE MASTER *throws on more incense. There is a flash and more copious smoke.)*

30. *A COUNTRY LANE NEAR THE BARROW.*

(THE DOCTOR *and* JO *are still tearing along in Bessie. Suddenly, without warning, a tree falls across the roadway just ahead of them.* THE DOCTOR *brings Bessie to a shuddering halt. They get out and try to shift the tree, but it is far too heavy.)*

THE DOCTOR: It's no good. It's wasting time. Come on, if we run, we'll just make it.

31. INTERIOR THE BARROW.

(PROFESSOR HORNER *is digging, and at the same time he addresses the camera.*)

HORNER: Let's face it, you've had enough blather from t'other fellow. You want to see for yourself. Well, I'll tell you what you're going to see. A stone wall.

(His trowel chinks against something solid.)

There you are, what did I tell you? I'm not daft.

(He begins to scrape the earth away from the stone.)

32. THE CAVERN.

(The cavern is now wreathed in smoke. The members of THE COVEN *keep up a constant moaning, circling the stone anti-clockwise.* THE MASTER'S *speech is now much more intense and the members of* THE COVEN *react vigorously.)*

COVEN: Io Evohe. Io Evohe. Io Evohe. Io Evohe...

THE MASTER: Ogot Erus Sawb Mal Taht! Tnew Yram Taht Ereh Wyr Evew Onssa Etih Wsawece Elfstib! Malelt Tilad Ahyram!

COVEN: Io Evohe!

THE MASTER: Eko Eko Azal!

COVEN: Eko Eko Azal!

(THE MASTER throws yet another substance on the thurible. There is a small explosion.)

33. Interior the Barrow.

(PROFESSOR HORNER *has almost reached the buried object.*)

34. Exterior the Barrow.

(THE DOCTOR *runs up the slope leading to the barrow.* JO *stumbles and is left far behind.*)

THE DOCTOR: Stop! Stop that dig! Stop it!

35. The Cavern.

THE MASTER: By the power of earth, by the power of the air, by the power of fire eternal and the waters of the deep, I conjure thee and charge thee, Azal, arise, arise. At my command, Azal, Azal...

COVEN: Azal!

36. Interior the Barrow.

(PROFESSOR HORNER *wrenches aside the stone, just as* THE DOCTOR *rushes down into the barrow.*)

THE DOCTOR: Stop! Don't pull that stone. Don't!

(*But he is too late. From the hole emerges a roaring noise, rising to a high scream. A blast of icy wind throws them to the ground.*)

37. Exterior the Barrow.

(*The whole area begins to shake, as if an earthquake has struck. The TV crew struggle to save their equipment. People panic and run, and there is general pandemonium.*)

38. *The Cavern.*

(THE MASTER *laughs in triumph as* THE COVEN
*cries out aloud in terror at the shaking of the
building. Suddenly,* GIRTON *points in horror at the
gargoyle, whose stone head is turning slowly
towards them, its eyes blazing a livid red.*)

THE MASTER: Azal!

GIRTON: Look!

39. *Exterior the Barrow.*

(*The wind, the earthquake and the noise continue
as* JO *struggles towards the barrow. She reaches
the entrance and goes in.*)

40. *Interior the Barrow.*

(*As* JO *enters she sees the bodies of* THE DOCTOR
and PROFESSOR HORNER *lying there, covered by a
strange kind of white frost.*)

JO: Doctor! Doctor! Are you all right? No!

(*As she leans over, an even stronger tremor
shakes the barrow and the earth face collapses,
burying* THE DOCTOR *and* PROFESSOR HORNER. JO
screams in horror.)

No! Oh Doctor, no!

EPISODE TWO

1. INTERIOR THE BARROW (NIGHT).

(PROFESSOR HORNER *wrenches aside the stone, just as* THE DOCTOR *rushes down into the barrow.*)

THE DOCTOR: Stop! Don't pull that stone. Don't!

(But he is too late. From the hole emerges a roaring noise, rising to a high scream. A blast of icy wind throws them to the ground.)

2. EXTERIOR THE BARROW.

(The whole area begins to shake, as if an earthquake has struck. The TV crew struggle to save their equipment. People panic and run, and there is general pandemonium.)

3. THE CAVERN.

(THE MASTER *laughs in triumph as* THE COVEN *cries out aloud in terror at the shaking of the building. Suddenly,* GIRTON *points in horror at the gargoyle, whose stone head is turning slowly towards them, its eyes blazing a livid red.*)

THE MASTER: Azal!

GIRTON: Look!

> 4. *EXTERIOR THE BARROW.*
>
> *(The wind, the earthquake and the noise continue as* JO *struggles towards the barrow. She reaches the entrance and goes in.)*

> 5. *INTERIOR THE BARROW.*
>
> *(As* JO *enters she sees the bodies of* THE DOCTOR *and* PROFESSOR HORNER *lying there, covered by a strange kind of white frost.)*

JO: Doctor! Doctor! Are you all right? No!

> *(As she leans over, an even stronger tremor shakes the barrow and the earth face collapses, burying* THE DOCTOR *and* PROFESSOR HORNER. JO *screams in horror.)*

        No! Oh Doctor, no!

> 6. *UNIT HQ DUTY ROOM.*
>
> *(*CAPTAIN YATES *and* SERGEANT BENTON *are still watching the rugby, which is just finishing.)*

YATES: Thirteen nil!

BENTON: Lucky it wasn't 113 nil! What a useless lot.

> *(*CAPTAIN YATES *holds out his hand and* BENTON *hands him the money for a lost bet.* YATES *looks at his watch and, realising the time, leaps to his feet.)*

YATES: We've missed the dig!

BENTON: Might just catch the end of it.

> *(He switches the television over. On the screen*

*the earth is shaking violently. The horrific noise
and icy wind continue.)*

YATES: Look, there's Jo!

*(She struggles into view on the television set and
begins frantically clawing at the fallen earth.)*

JO: Doctor!

*(Suddenly, the picture vanishes and a hastily-
assembled sign replaces it. 'Devil's End.
Temporary fault. BBC-3 TV'.)*

ANNOUNCER We seem to have lost all contact with the barrow.
(*oov*): We shall, of course, resume transmission as soon as
we can. In the meantime, here is some music...

YATES: Benton, get onto the BBC and see if you can find out
what's going on down there. I'll try to raise the
Brigadier.

BENTON: Right, sir.

7. *INTERIOR THE BARROW.*

*(The noise and movement are subsiding now. JO
has been joined by a couple of others, and together they start to uncover THE DOCTOR's head. JO is
weeping uncontrollably.)*

JO: Look, hurry! Please hurry!

8. *THE CAVERN.*

*(Although the shaking has stopped, THE COVEN is
still in a state of terror, on their knees. THE MAS-
TER stands triumphantly before the stone of sacrifice.)*

THE MASTER:	O Great Azal, I, the Master, thank thee for arising at my command. Behold my worthy disciples. They know now of thy presence and will seek to help thee fulfil my desires. Therefore, I command them to rise to their feet and welcome thee, Azal.

(The members of THE COVEN *struggle to their feet.)*

	To do my will shall be the whole of the law.
COVEN:	To do thy will shall be the whole of the law.
THE MASTER:	Azal. Hear me...

(He walks around the stone, pointing the sacrificial knife towards it.)

	Let this stone mark the appointed place. Let us meet together later, that thou mayest learn of my intent. As my will, so mote it be.
COVEN:	As thy will, so mote it be.
THE MASTER:	You have nothing to fear as long as you do the will of the Master. Go now and say no word to any man, and await my commands.

(THE COVEN, *still terrified, begin to file out into the vestry.)*

9. *INTERIOR THE BARROW.*

(PROFESSOR HORNER *and* THE DOCTOR *have now both been uncovered. They are frozen stiff and totally lifeless.* HARRY *is examining* THE DOCTOR, *having established that* THE PROFESSOR *is dead.)*

HARRY:	He's gone, too.

JO: No! No, he can't be! We must get a doctor.

HARRY: Look, love, face it. They've had it.

JO: But there must be a doctor in the village or somewhere.

     (HARRY *shouts to someone at the entrance to the barrow*.)

HARRY: Charlie! Can I have a word with you a minute?

     (He turns to JO.)

     Charlie'll take 'em down, love.

JO: Thank you. Doctor... Doctor, please...

     10. UNIT HQ DUTY ROOM.

     (YATES *and* BENTON *are speaking simultaneously on two separate phones*.)

BENTON: Now listen, this is an official call from UNIT... United Nations Intelligence Taskforce... I warn you, if you're withholding information, I'll... You must know something... Well, find out and ring me back at this number.

     (He replaces the receiver.)

YATES: Right then, I'll ring you back. Ten minutes... no, make it five.

     (He slams down the phone.)

     Anything?

BENTON: No, sir. You?

YATES: No. The Brigadier went on somewhere after the dinner. No one knows quite where.

ANNOUNCER
(*oov*):
Well, we're very sorry for this interruption in our outside broadcast from Devil's End, but we still can't get through to our unit at the dig, but as soon as we have some news...

YATES:
This is stupid! I've a good mind to go down there and find out for myself.

BENTON:
The Brigadier'd go spare, sir. I mean, we might get news at any minute.

YATES:
Oh yes, sure. And in the meantime, what's happening to Jo and the Doctor?

(He gets up and starts to leave.)

11. THE CLOVEN HOOF PUB.

(DOCTOR REEVES *is examining* THE DOCTOR.)

REEVES:
Too late, I'm afraid. He's gone... just like the Professor.

JO:
No, no! He can't be dead.

REEVES:
I'm sorry.

JO:
Please, you must do something.

REEVES:
I can't work miracles, you know. He's very nearly a solid block of ice.

(JO *turns away in tears.* WINSTANLEY *comforts her.)*

WINSTANLEY:
There, there... I'm sorry, my dear. There's nothing we can do.

REEVES:
Good grief!

WINSTANLEY:
What?

REEVES:
Get some blankets and some hot water bottles... lots of them.

BERT: Right, doctor.

JO: He's alive then?

REEVES: It's impossible, but I think I felt a pulse.

JO: There's a chance.

REEVES: Maybe. He must have the constitution of an ox to be able to survive a reduction of temperature like that.

WINSTANLEY: Doesn't look all that tough.

                (REEVES *is now listening to* THE DOCTOR*'s chest with his stethoscope.*)

REEVES: You can't always tell by... Hello?

JO: What?

REEVES: Silly, really. I could swear it sounds as if he's... It's quite ridiculous. It must be an echo of an atypical bone structure.

WINSTANLEY: Sounds as if what?

REEVES: As if he has two hearts - one on each side.

                (BERT *brings in some blankets.*)

                Fine, fine. Now more if you've got them.

                (He starts to wrap the blankets around THE DOCTOR.*)*

JO: He's going to be all right, then?

REEVES: There is a chance.

WINSTANLEY: Cheer up. Where there's life, there's hope.. Right?

                (JO *gives him a watery smile and looks at* BERT.)

JO: Have you got a phone I could use, please?

BERT:	In the corner.
JO:	Oh yes. Thank you.

12. UNIT HQ DUTY ROOM.

(YATES *is on the phone, talking to* JO.)

YATES:	But is he all right now?

13. THE CLOVEN HOOF PUB.

JO:	Well, it's touch and go, I think. Mike, look, can you get down here, right away?

14. UNIT HQ DUTY ROOM.

YATES:	Yes, of course. We'll come down in the chopper as soon as it's light.

15. THE CELLAR.

(As JO *and* YATES *are talking, an anonymous hand cuts the telephone cable.*)

16. UNIT HQ DUTY ROOM.

YATES:	Hello? Jo? Can you hear me? Blast! We've been cut off.

17. EXTERIOR THE BARROW.

(*The last BBC vehicle moves away.* HARRY *is inside the landrover. He stops by* PC GROOM, *at the gate.*)

HARRY: Well, that's the last of us. Thanks for all your help.

PC GROOM: Happy to oblige, sir.

HARRY: I can't wait to get away myself. I don't envy you.

PC GROOM: Oh that's all right, sir. Just a bit of night duty. I enjoy a bit of peace and quiet.

HARRY: Well, you're welcome to it, mate. Anyway, I'm away. 'Night.

PC GROOM: Bye, sir.

(As they drive away, PC GROOM *shuts the gate behind them and places a large 'Danger' sign on it. Then he settles down, taking out a packet of sandwiches. Behind him, from the entrance to the barrow a pair of malevolent red eyes watch him.)*

18. THE CLOVEN HOOF PUB (DAWN).

*(*THE DOCTOR *is in bed, unconscious.* JO *is anxiously watching him.)*

19. THE CAVERN.

*(*THE MASTER *is alone. He approaches the altar, raises his arms and, taking on an intense look of concentration, begins to mutter an invocation.)*

20. EXTERIOR THE BARROW.

*(*PC GROOM *suddenly feels uncomfortable. He looks round in terror, as the ground starts to shake. He screams and falls to the ground. Something crushes the life out of him and continues on its way.)*

21. The Cavern.

(THE MASTER *opens his eyes with a look of satisfaction and leaves the cavern.*)

22. The Countryside (Day).

(*The UNIT helicopter sweeps across the sky.*)

23. Interior UNIT Helicopter.

(CAPTAIN YATES *and* SERGEANT BENTON *are in the helicopter.* BENTON *is piloting, while* YATES *navigates.*)

BENTON: Soon be there, sir.

YATES: Hello, what's that?

(YATES *takes off his sunglasses and stares in amazement at the ground below.*)

BENTON: Must be the dig.

YATES: No, beyond that. A line of... they couldn't be hoofmarks, could they? They're enormous!

BENTON: Shall we go and see, sir?

YATES: Better.

24. A Field.

(*The helicopter lands.* YATES *and* BENTON *jump out and go over to examine the giant indentations.*)

BENTON: They are you know, sir. Hoofmarks!

YATES: But they can't be. The animal that made these would have to be at least thirty feet tall.

BENTON: Oh well, whatever it is, it's gone into that wood, over there.

YATES: It'll have to wait. Come on. First things first.

BENTON: What, like breakfast you mean, sir?

YATES: No, I don't. I mean Jo and the Doc.

            (*They make their way back to the helicopter.*)

            25. THE CLOVEN HOOF PUB.

            (JO, *still sitting by the unconscious form of* THE DOCTOR, *has nodded off to sleep. The sound of the helicopter awakens her and, overjoyed, she rushes to the window.*)

            26. THE VILLAGE GREEN.

            (*The helicopter lands on the green.*)

            27. THE CLOVEN HOOF PUB.

            (JO *turns and runs out of the room.*)

            28. THE VILLAGE GREEN.

            (YATES *and* BENTON *get out of the helicopter.*)

BENTON: Where's the red carpet, then? And the brass band.

YATES: After last night I reckon we all deserve a lie-in.

BENTON: There's the pub, sir.

YATES: And Jo.

            (JO *comes running towards them.*)

29. THE CLOVEN HOOF PUB.

(JO, YATES and BENTON *all enter the public house.*)

YATES:	You're sure you're all right?
JO:	Yes thanks. Honest. Boy, am I glad to see you two.
YATES:	And the Doc?
JO:	Upstairs. Better, I think. But he's still out cold.
YATES:	Oh, he'll pull through. You know what a tough old bird he is.
BENTON:	Anyway, you're both safe, that's the main thing.
JO:	I don't think there's any danger in here. But out there...
YATES:	Look, Jo... what *is* going on?
JO:	I... I don't know. Something really bad. You know?
YATES:	Well, how d'you mean?
JO:	Well, you know... Devilish.
BENTON:	Look sir, if you don't need me here, I'd like to make a quick recce of those tracks.
YATES:	Oh...
BENTON:	Look, fifteen minutes... say twenty.
YATES:	Right. But at the first sign of trouble, straight back here.
BENTON:	Right.
JO:	Do be careful, Sergeant Benton.
BENTON:	Don't you worry, miss. Oh... and don't forget to contact the Brigadier, sir.
YATES:	Agh! I'd forgotten all about him!

30. THE BRIGADIER'S BEDROOM.

(THE BRIGADIER *is in bed, speaking on the telephone. He has clearly been woken up by the call.*)

BRIGADIER: The Doctor's gone? Gone where... Well, you should know, Corporal, I want to talk to him... What? All right then, wake up Miss Grant... I see, and I suppose she didn't leave a number, either? I suppose it wouldn't do any good to ask for Captain Yates or Sergeant Benton? My helicopter! Where to? Devil's End? Yes, yes, I see. Get my car here right away. Yes... and if they do contact you, tell them to stay put!

31. THE CHURCHYARD.

(BENTON *is cutting through the churchyard on his way to the wood. As he passes the vestry door, he hears a faint cry for help. He goes to investigate.*)

32. THE VESTRY.

(BENTON *quickly locates the source of the cry - a large chest. He pulls the lid open and finds* MISS HAWTHORNE *inside. He helps her out.*)

HAWTHORNE: Oh! Friend or foe?

BENTON: Friend, I hope, ma'am.

HAWTHORNE: A very perfect gentle knight.

BENTON: What?

HAWTHORNE: Your damsel in distress may be a bit long in the tooth, but... she's very grateful.

BENTON: Well yes, you're lucky I heard you.

HAWTHORNE: Who are you?

(BENTON *is just finishing untying her.*)

BENTON: Benton. Sergeant Benton. What happened?

HAWTHORNE: A police sergeant?

BENTON: No, army. Now who put you in here?

HAWTHORNE: Garvin... the verger. We must... we must get the police at once. My name's Olive Hawthorne by the way. How do you do.

BENTON: How do you do. Look, what is going on here? All hell seems to be breaking loose.

HAWTHORNE: You know, Sergeant, you're exactly right. Come on.

(*She opens the door but immediately holds up a hand to warn* BENTON *to keep quiet.*)

Ssssh!

BENTON: What is it?

33. THE CHURCHYARD.

(*He looks through the crack in the door.* GARVIN, *although some distance away, is approaching the vestry.*)

34. THE VESTRY.

HAWTHORNE: Garvin. The one who tied me up.

(*She gently closes the door.*)

Quickly...

(*She leads them over to the cavern door.*)

We can hide down here until he's out of the way.

(BENTON *goes down the steps.* MISS HAWTHORNE *follows him, closing the door quietly.)*

35. *THE CAVERN.*

(They come down the steps into the cavern.)

HAWTHORNE: Good heavens!

BENTON: What? What is it?

(She points to the empty recess.)

HAWTHORNE: The gargoyle. It's gone!

(A door slams shut above and footsteps approach.)

Ssssh!

(MISS HAWTHORNE *beckons* BENTON *into an alcove.* GARVIN *opens the door to the cavern, comes in and looks around. After a moment, he withdraws, closing the door as he does.* BENTON *starts to move, but* MISS HAWTHORNE *restrains him.)*

Better wait until he's gone.

(BENTON *notices a curiously marked flagstone on the floor of the cavern.)*

BENTON: Here, what's this?

(MISS HAWTHORNE *examines it.)*

HAWTHORNE: The sign of the Evil One.

(BENTON *looks closely.)*

Keep away!

BENTON:	For goodness' sake!
HAWTHORNE:	You know who's at the bottom of all this?
BENTON:	No, who?
HAWTHORNE:	The Reverend Mr Magister.
BENTON:	Who's he?
HAWTHORNE:	The vicar... so-called. But he's an imposter.
BENTON:	Oh yeah?
HAWTHORNE:	Oh, I should have realised at once. Magister is the name given to the leader of a black magic coven.

(She crosses to the altar, followed by BENTON.*)*

BENTON:	Black magic? That stuff died out years ago.
HAWTHORNE:	Do you know when the last witchcraft act was repealed in this country? 1951... It is alive today as it ever was.
BENTON:	Yes, well...
HAWTHORNE:	It should be safe now.
GARVIN (*oov*):	That's what you think!

(He comes into view, carrying a shotgun, which he points at them.)

Move it. On your way. Move.

(They turn. Without warning, BENTON *leaps on* GARVIN *and knocks the gun flying. They grapple with each other, and as they roll over each other on the floor,* GARVIN *manages to push* BENTON *onto the marked flagstone. Immediately he is*

assailed by a hundred invisible fists. Vainly fighting the empty air, he is beaten to the ground. MISS HAWTHORNE *rushes to help him and drags him from the flagstone.*)

All right, on your feet.

HAWTHORNE: Don't be stupid. Can't you see he's half unconscious?

GARVIN: Somebody'll have to help him then, won't they?

(He points the gun at MISS HAWTHORNE *and she sees that she has no choice.)*

Right. Come on. This way.

36. A BEDROOM AT THE CLOVEN HOOF PUB.

(YATES *leans over* THE DOCTOR.)

YATES: Doctor... Doctor... wake up.

(There is no reaction.)

JO: You see. He's been like that for hours.

YATES: Well, shouldn't he be in hospital?

JO: Doctor Reeves said that we shouldn't move him.

YATES: Then we'll just have to wait.

37. THE CHURCHYARD.

(GARVIN *cautiously opens the main door of the church. Seeing the coast is clear, he turns and gestures to* MISS HAWTHORNE *to bring* BENTON *out. As they move off down the path round the church there is a thudding sound of mighty footsteps and the ground begins to shake.* GARVIN *and* MISS HAWTHORNE *turn to look and stare in terror at what they see. A huge shadow falls over them and the church, and* GARVIN *forgets his captives. He retreats towards the church door and* MISS HAWTHORNE *drags* BENTON *behind a nearby tombstone. A strange whistling sound is heard and an orange glow seems to light the very air.* GARVIN *raises his gun and fires. There is a sudden flash and he disappears, vaporised into nothingness.)*

38. *A BEDROOM AT THE CLOVEN HOOF PUB.*

(The whole room is shaking violently as JO *and* YATES *struggle to keep their balance. Suddenly, a wave of pure heat envelopes them.)*

39. *THE CAVERN.*

(The thud of heavy feet can still be heard. It approaches the church and starts to move down into the cavern. As it reaches the flagstone, the heat begins to fade and the shaking and the noise both stop.)

40. *A BEDROOM AT THE CLOVEN HOOF PUB.*

(In the sudden silence which follows, YATES *and* JO *pick themselves up. Suddenly* THE DOCTOR *sits bolt upright in bed.)*

THE DOCTOR: Eureka!

41. The Vicarage.

THE MASTER: Azal! I welcome thee.

42. A Country Road.

(A baker's van is coming down the road. Suddenly, the ground begins to shake and the wind begins to rise. The driver of the van fights to control it as it bucks and veers across the road. The strange noise gets louder and louder. He jumps out of the van and, as he staggers away, the van suddenly explodes in a ball of flame. The noise recedes, leaving the terrified man shaking his head in disbelief.)

43. The Cloven Hoof Pub.

(THE DOCTOR *comes down the stairs, followed by* YATES *and* JO.)

JO: But are you sure you're all right? Look, you'd better come and sit in this chair. Come on. Over here.

THE DOCTOR: Jo... Jo, please... stop fussing.

YATES: She's right, you know. Better take it gently.

THE DOCTOR: Look, I tell you I am perfectly all right. It was a bit parky up there for a while, I'll admit, but it soon warmed up.

JO: That wave of heat?

THE DOCTOR: Yes, the final confirmation of my theory.

JO: You mean, you know what caused it?

THE DOCTOR: Yes, I think so.

YATES: Tell us then.

THE DOCTOR: No, not just yet. I want to wait until I'm absolutely sure. Right, I'm going back up to the dig.

JO: Doctor, haven't you had enough of that place?

(BERT *comes in behind the bar.*)

BERT: Hullo - you better? I thought you'd had it.

THE DOCTOR: Fortunately, no. Captain Yates, you'd better wait here, all right?

(*The door is suddenly flung open and* MISS HAWTHORNE *staggers in, half-dragging the semi-conscious* SERGEANT BENTON. *For a moment everyone is too stunned to move.*)

HAWTHORNE: If I drop him, he'll go a most dreadful wallop.

(THE DOCTOR *and* YATES *leap into action.*)

YATES: He's out on his feet.

THE DOCTOR: Get him over to that bench. Quickly.

BERT: Whatever's happened to you, boy?

(BENTON *groans.*)

YATES: He's been beaten up. By an expert, I'd say.

HAWTHORNE: You might indeed say that... you might indeed!

(*She sinks into a chair, exhausted.*)

Oh dear, oh dear. He's a very heavy young man.

BERT: I'll get a doctor.

THE DOCTOR: Yes all right, I am a doctor.

(*He starts to examine* BENTON.)

Well, there are no bones broken, at any rate. Look, could you get me some hot water, and some hot sweet tea perhaps?

BERT: Yes, certainly.

THE DOCTOR: Thank you very much... and thank you too, Miss Hawthorne.

HAWTHORNE: You know who I am?

THE DOCTOR: Well yes, of course. It's a great pity they didn't listen to you in the first place.

HAWTHORNE: If only they had. Oh, what a tale I'll have to tell them now.

44. THE VICARAGE.

(THE MASTER *is speaking on the phone. It is not clear to whom he is speaking.*)

THE MASTER: Both alive, are they? And the others?... I see. Very well, they'll all be dealt with. Now you'd better get back inside before they become suspicious.

45. THE CLOVEN HOOF PUB.

YATES: So it was this fellow Garvin who did him over?

HAWTHORNE: No, no, no! It was the elementals... in the cavern.

THE DOCTOR: Elementals?

HAWTHORNE: Yes... creatures of the Devil.

YATES: Did you say the Devil?

HAWTHORNE:	Yes, dear boy. Satan, Lucifer, the Prince of Darkness, Beelzebub, the Horned Beast; call him what you like. He was there.
THE DOCTOR:	You saw the Devil? Well what did he look like?
HAWTHORNE:	Well, it was a glimpse, no more, Twenty... thirty feet high. But the horns were there, and that face!
JO:	The Devil!
THE DOCTOR:	Miss Hawthorne, I've agreed with you from the first about the danger. But now I think you're utterly mistaken. Whatever else you saw, it certainly was not the Devil.
HAWTHORNE:	But it was. There's a Satanist cult in the village, and last night they held a Sabbat.
YATES:	A Sabbat?
HAWTHORNE:	Yes, an occult ceremony. To call up the Devil.
JO:	And it worked... the Devil came!
THE DOCTOR:	Nonsense, Jo. Miss Hawthorne, who is the leader of this cult?
HAWTHORNE:	The new vicar. He calls himself Magister.
THE DOCTOR:	Magister! Yes, of course. I should have known.
JO:	What?
	(As they are talking BERT *comes back in carrying a tray with the things that* THE DOCTOR *had requested.)*
THE DOCTOR:	Jo, did you fail Latin as well as science? Magister is the Latin word for Master!

46. A Country Road.

(THE BRIGADIER, *in a UNIT car, is flagged down by the hapless* BAKER, *standing by his burnt-out van.*)

BRIGADIER: What's up?

BAKER: I shouldn't go any further, mate. Look what's happened to my van.

               (THE BRIGADIER *gets out and walks forward.*)

BRIGADIER: Petrol fire?

BAKER: No. Just went up in a flash.

               (*On either side of the van, stretching away as far as the eye can see, is a band of scorched earth, some fifteen feet wide.*)

BRIGADIER: During the earth tremors, was it?

BAKER: No. Just after it stopped. I was about to get back in and drive on to the village and... bingo! Up it went.

BRIGADIER: Is that Devil's End over there?

               (*As he speaks he gestures towards the village with his baton, the end of which suddenly bursts into flame.*)

BAKER: That's right... Blimey!

               (THE BRIGADIER, *having put out the flames, cautiously approaches and again raises the baton. It bursts into flame once more.*)

BRIGADIER: A heat barrier. We'll try and get in from the south.

47. THE ROAD TO THE DIG.

THE DOCTOR: Right.

(THE DOCTOR *and* JO *move the last piece of tree away from Bessie's path.*)

Get the saw, would you?

(JO *picks up the saw they have been using and they climb into Bessie and drive off.*)

48. A COUNTRY ROAD.

(THE BRIGADIER*'s car stops just before a blackened line across the road in front of them. He and his driver get out.* THE BRIGADIER *picks up a twig and tosses it towards the line. It bursts into flame and is instantly consumed.*)

BRIGADIER: Now that settles it. We'd better try and raise the Doctor.

49. THE CLOVEN HOOF PUB.

YATES: ... and that's about it, sir. Over.

50. A COUNTRY ROAD.

BRIGADIER: I see, Yates. So the Doctor was frozen stiff at the barrow and was then revived by a freak heatwave. Benton was beaten up by invisible forces and the local white witch claims she's seen the Devil?

YATES (*oov*):   Yes, sir. I know it sounds a bit wild.

BRIGADIER: It does indeed, Yates. Now listen. I'm bringing up some men to investigate this heat barrier. Let me talk to the Doctor. Over.

51. THE CLOVEN HOOF PUB.

YATES: I'm afraid you can't, sir. He's gone up to the dig with Jo. Over.

BRIGADIER (*oov*): I see. Well, Yates, any further revelations?

YATES: Just one, sir.

52. A COUNTRY ROAD.

BRIGADIER: Well, what is it?

YATES (*oov*): We've found out who's at the bottom of all this. It's the Master. Over and out.

53. THE VICARAGE.

THE MASTER: Still alive are you, Doctor? Very well.

(*He throws back his head and closes his eyes. There is a strange chattering noise and the sound of beating wings outside.* THE MASTER *goes to the window and looks into the sky beyond.*)

54. A COUNTRY LANE NEAR THE BARROW.

(*Bessie speeds along a lane towards the barrow.* THE DOCTOR *spots something lying in the road ahead and stops the car. They get out and discover the crushed body of* PC GROOM.)

THE DOCTOR: Poor fellow.

JO: You know what killed him?

THE DOCTOR: Well, it certainly wasn't the Devil. At least, not exactly.

JO: What do you mean?

THE DOCTOR: Look, I'm going in. Would you prefer to wait outside?

JO: No, I'd rather stick with you, if I wouldn't be in the way.

THE DOCTOR: No, of course not. I'd be glad of the company.

(As they go down into the barrow, something is watching them from the hillside above.)

55. INTERIOR THE BARROW.

JO: What are you looking for?

THE DOCTOR: If my theory's right, we're all in mortal danger.

JO: Everyone in the village?

THE DOCTOR: Everyone in the whole world. Ah!

(He sees something lying on the floor of the barrow and crouches down to examine it.)

56. EXTERIOR THE BARROW.

(BOK, the gargoyle, runs down the hillside towards the entrance to the barrow.)

57. INTERIOR THE BARROW.

(THE DOCTOR is busy digging in the soft earth that has recently fallen. He soon finds what he is looking for.)

JO: What is it?

THE DOCTOR: Metal.

JO: Looks like a model spaceship.

THE DOCTOR: That's right. Except that it isn't a model.

JO: What is it then?

THE DOCTOR: Jo, look at the shape of this tomb.

JO: Well, it looks like that spaceship.

THE DOCTOR: A different size, that's all. Now you try picking it up.

(She tries in vain.)

JO: I can't. It's fixed down.

THE DOCTOR: The reason why you can't pick it up is that it weighs... about 750 tons, at a rough guess.

JO: Oh come on, be serious.

THE DOCTOR: Be serious... all right, about a 100,000 years ago...

58. Exterior the Barrow.

(BOK approaches the entrance to the barrow. As the gargoyle enters it lets out a great roar.)

59. Interior the Barrow.

(As BOK roars, THE DOCTOR and JO turn and see it for the first time. They back away as its eyes blaze red in the gloom. It gives another roar and JO screams.)

EPISODE THREE

1. EXTERIOR THE BARROW (DAY).

(BOK, *the gargoyle, runs down the hillside towards the entrance to the barrow.*)

2. INTERIOR THE BARROW.

(THE DOCTOR *is busy digging in the soft earth that has recently fallen. He soon finds what he is looking for.*)

JO: What is it?

THE DOCTOR: Metal.

JO: Looks like a model spaceship.

THE DOCTOR: That's right. Except that it isn't a model.

JO: What is it then?

THE DOCTOR: Jo, look at the shape of this tomb.

JO: Well, it looks like that spaceship.

THE DOCTOR: A different size, that's all. Now you try picking it up.

(*She tries in vain.*)

JO: I can't. It's fixed down.

THE DOCTOR: The reason why you can't pick it up is that it weighs... about 750 tons, at a rough guess.

JO: Oh come on, be serious.

THE DOCTOR: Be serious... all right, about a 100,000 years ago...

> 3. *EXTERIOR THE BARROW.*
>
> (BOK *approaches the entrance to the barrow. As the gargoyle enters it gives a great roar.*)
>
> 4. *INTERIOR THE BARROW.*
>
> (*As* BOK *roars,* THE DOCTOR *and* JO *turn and see it for the first time. They back away as its eyes blaze red in the gloom. It gives another roar and* JO *screams.*)

THE DOCTOR: Be quiet, Jo. Hold this.

> (*He passes her the torch.* BOK *advances slowly, raising his arms in a menacing gesture. Suddenly,* THE DOCTOR *shoots out his right hand, holding in it a small trowel which he points at* BOK.)

Klokleda partha mennin klatch!

> (BOK *recoils with a snarl.*)
>
> 5. *THE VICARAGE.*
>
> (THE MASTER *stands with his eyes closed. He frowns and opens them. He puts his head back and the chattering noise is heard once more.*)
>
> 6. *INTERIOR THE BARROW.*
>
> (BOK, *still held at bay, raises his snout and chatters back.*)

7. *THE VICARAGE*.

THE MASTER: What's happening, Bok? Why do you not attack?

8. *INTERIOR THE BARROW*.

(Again BOK *chatters.)*

9. *THE VICARAGE*.

THE MASTER: But you must. You must! There's nothing to fear in such mumbo-jumbo, I... Oh very well, return. Return!

10. *INTERIOR THE BARROW*.

*(*BOK *chatters one last time, and then turns and goes. We hear the heavy sound of his wings.)*

THE DOCTOR: Whew!

JO: How did you do that?

*(*THE DOCTOR *holds up the trowel.)*

THE DOCTOR: Iron. It's an old magical defence.

JO: But you don't believe in magic!

THE DOCTOR: I don't. But he did... luckily!

JO: And was that a spell you said?

THE DOCTOR: No, it was the first line of an old Venusian lullaby, as a matter of fact. Roughly translated, it goes 'Close your eyes my darling, well three of them at least...'

*(*JO *laughs in spite of her terror.)*

JO: Doctor!

THE DOCTOR:	I must admit... that thing took me completely by surprise.
JO:	What was it?
THE DOCTOR:	It looked like a gargoyle. Made of stone.
JO:	But it was alive!
THE DOCTOR:	In a sense, yes.
JO:	But that wasn't what Miss Hawthorne described, surely?
THE DOCTOR:	No. The creature she saw must have been a hundred times more hideous.
JO:	But neither of them were... the Devil?
THE DOCTOR:	No, not your mythical Devil, Jo, no. Something far more real... and far more dangerous.

11. THE VICARAGE.

(THE MASTER *is talking to the squire,* WINSTANLEY.)

THE MASTER:	Now see here, Winstanley. This is an emergency. It's up to you to call a meeting of the village and start behaving like the Squire.
WINSTANLEY:	You may be the vicar, but I'll thank you not to take that tone with me.
THE MASTER:	Ah! A man of spirit, are you? That's exactly what's wanted at a time like this.
WINSTANLEY:	I still don't understand what you're talking about.
THE MASTER:	Decadence! That's what I'm talking about. That's what I see on every side. All this talk of democracy...

freedom... liberty. What this country needs is strength, power and decision. And those are what you can give to it.

(As he talks, THE MASTER *stares into the squire's eyes, trying to hypnotise him.)*

WINSTANLEY: Yes... yes. You're right, of course...

*(*THE MASTER *relaxes his gaze, thinking that he has the squire under control.)*

THE MASTER: I am the Master! I control a power which can save this world. If you choose, you can share my triumph!

WINSTANLEY: Power? What power?

*(*THE MASTER *frowns, realising that this is not as easy as he had expected.)*

THE MASTER: I control the forces that have been released in Devil's End over the last few hours.

WINSTANLEY: All that fuss up on the dig? Are you trying to tell me it was you?

THE MASTER: Exactly.

WINSTANLEY: But that is ridiculous!

THE MASTER: You need proof, do you? Very well, you shall have it!

(He closes his eyes and lifts his head. Immediately there is a whining sound and the room seems to spring to life. Doors and windows fly open and slam shut; pictures fall; chairs and tables are overturned. WINSTANLEY *is terrified.)*

WINSTANLEY: Stop it! Stop it!

(THE MASTER *opens his eyes and the room quickly subsides.*)

THE MASTER: Well?

WINSTANLEY: I'll do anything you say.

12. *THE CLOVEN HOOF PUB.*

(MISS HAWTHORNE *staggers in with a pile of books, pictures and transparencies. She dumps them down.* YATES *follows her in with a projector.* BENTON *is recovering, but still resting on a couch.*)

HAWTHORNE: Here you are, Doctor.

THE DOCTOR: Oh thank you, Miss Hawthorne. Let me help you.

HAWTHORNE: Thank you. Pick of the finest collection of occult material in the country. Though why you wanted me to bring it, I don't know.

THE DOCTOR: You've all been asking me for explanations. Perhaps these will help me to provide them.

HAWTHORNE: There is only one possible explanation. This is the supernatural at work!

THE DOCTOR: Nonsense!

BENTON: Yes, well what about the thing that got me? That was real enough.

THE DOCTOR: There's nothing more real than a force-field, Sergeant... even a psionic one.

HAWTHORNE: Oh, you're being deliberately obtuse. We are dealing with the supernatural. The occult! Magic!

THE DOCTOR: Science.

HAWTHORNE:	Magic!
THE DOCTOR:	Science, Miss Hawthorne.
YATES:	Look, whatever it is, how do we stop it?
JO:	How can we stop it without knowing what it is?
THE DOCTOR:	Well done, Jo! You're being logical at last. I'll turn you into a scientist yet. Right, if there are no more interruptions, I'll tell you what it is...

(YATES' *walkie-talkie bleeps.*)

YATES: Sorry... Greyhound Two. Come in please. Over.

13. UNIT MOBILE HQ.

BRIGADIER: Greyhound Two to Trap Two. Is that you, Yates? Now what's going on there?

YATES (*oov*):   Quite a bit. But I don't think you'd believe me, even if I told you.

BRIGADIER: The thing is, we can't get past this wretched heat barrier. It incinerates anything that tries. Over.

14. THE CLOVEN HOOF PUB.

YATES: Can't you go round it, Brigadier? Over.

15. UNIT MOBILE HQ.

BRIGADIER: The thought had occurred to me, Captain. I've sent out patrols, and as far as I can see...

(*One of his men,* OSGOOD, *hands him a piece of paper.*)

Well that settles it. The perimeter of this thing is an unbroken circle, ten miles...

16. THE CLOVEN HOOF PUB.

... in diameter, it's centre being the village church. Over.

THE DOCTOR: Give me that.

(THE DOCTOR *grabs the walkie-talkie from* CAPTAIN YATES.)

Hello, Lethbridge-Stewart? The Doctor here. What about going over the top of it?

17. UNIT MOBILE HQ.

BRIGADIER: The RAF are just coming through now. Hang on a minute.

(He gets up.)

18. EXTERIOR UNIT MOBILE HQ.

(Up in the sky, a Strike Command plane homes in on its target.)

19. UNIT MOBILE HQ.

(A distorted voice has just started to come through on the radio transmitter. THE BRIGADIER turns his attention back to that.)

VOICE (*oov*): Red Zero-Four to Greyhound Two. No soap, repeat, no soap. Last test canister exploded at altitude four-five-zero-zero feet. Estimate dome-shaped barrier

	above village approximately one mile high at apogee. Over.
OSGOOD:	Thank you, Zero-Four. Received and understood.
VOICE (*oov*):	Over and out.
BRIGADIER:	You hear that, Doctor? We're locked out. Over.

20. *THE CLOVEN HOOF PUB.*

THE DOCTOR: Or we're locked in. All right, Brigadier. We'll keep in touch.

(*He switches the walkie-talkie off.*)

21. *UNIT MOBILE HQ.*

BRIGADIER: Doctor? Doctor! Yates? Typical!

22. *THE CLOVEN HOOF PUB.*

THE DOCTOR: Right... that's it.

(*He has sketched an outline of the dome-shaped heat-barrier on a piece of paper.*)

Now, as you can see, we're smack in the middle of a sort of lethal mushroom... about ten miles across and a mile high.

YATES: I can understand that part of it all right, but can't you explain the wider issues, Doctor?

THE DOCTOR: Yes, all right. Jo, Captain Yates, would you mind drawing the curtains? Come on Jo, stir your stumps.

(*He takes some transparencies and puts them in the projector. The first image appears on the screen.*)

	Now then, all right? Now then, tell me who's that?
JO:	An Egyptian God, isn't it?
THE DOCTOR:	Top of the class, Jo. Top of the class, that's right. That's the Egyptian God Khnun... with horns.

(He changes the slide.)

And there's another one... A Hindu demon...

(The others all chorus in unison.)

JO, YATES, BENTON & HAWTHORNE:	With horns!
THE DOCTOR:	Oh! Thank you very much.

(He changes the slide again, this time to a classic image of... the Devil.)

And our old friend, the Horned Beast...

YATES:	I don't get it.
THE DOCTOR:	Probably because I haven't finished, Captain Yates.
YATES:	Oh, sorry Doctor.
HAWTHORNE:	You could go on all day and all night showing us pretty pictures. I mean horns have been a symbol of power ever since...

(THE DOCTOR *projects another slide.*)

THE DOCTOR:	Ever since man began? Exactly... but why? All right, Captain Yates. The curtains.

(As THE DOCTOR *switches off the projector,* CAPTAIN YATES *pulls open the curtains.)*

Now creatures like those have been seen over and over again throughout the history of man... and man has turned them into myths... Gods... or Devils. But they are neither. They are, in fact, creatures from another world.

BENTON: You mean like the Axons... and the Cybermen?

THE DOCTOR: Precisely. Only far, far older, and immeasurably more dangerous!

JO: And they came here in space ships? Like that tiny one up at the barrow?

THE DOCTOR: That's right. They're Daemons... from the planet Damos, which is...

JO: 60,000 light years away, on the other side of the galaxy.

THE DOCTOR: And they first came to Earth... nearly 100,000 years ago.

23. THE VICARAGE.

(The room is crowded with people from the village. THE MASTER *murmurs into* WINSTANLEY's *ear.)*

THE MASTER: You'd better explain to them all why you've called them together; then leave the rest to me.

WINSTANLEY: Yes, yes, of course.

(THE VILLAGERS, *who include members of* THE COVEN, *are busy talking amongst themselves.)*

Meeting to order, please! Thank you. Thank you, ladies and gentlemen.

(The talking quickly subsides.)

Well now, it seemed to me that we ought to get

together and discuss the situation, before it gets out of hand. Now it seems that the vicar here has had a few thoughts on the subject... so I've asked him to put in a word. Mr Magister?

THE MASTER: Thank you.

(THE MASTER *steps forward. He waits until there is absolute silence before starting to address the crowd.*)

24. *THE CLOVEN HOOF PUB.*

JO: A space ship fifteen inches long?

THE DOCTOR: That's right. Mind you, when it landed it was two hundred feet long and thirty feet across. But they diminished it... just as they diminish themselves. Which accounts for the heatwave and the freeze-up.

JO: Sorry, could you say that again? I didn't quite follow you.

THE DOCTOR: Oh, come on, Jo! $E = MC^2$.

JO: You're the Doctor.

THE DOCTOR: Look, when you lose mass, the energy has to go somewhere.

YATES: I see. So all we've got to deal with is something which is either too small to see or thirty feet tall, can incinerate you or freeze you to death, turns stone images into homicidal monsters... and looks like the very Devil.

THE DOCTOR: Exactly.

BENTON: Well, I still don't get it. I mean, what's the creature doing here? I mean why did they ever come?

THE DOCTOR: To help Homosapiens take out Neanderthal man... they've been coming and going ever since. The Greek civilisation, the Renaissance, the Industrial Revolution... they were all inspired by the Daemons.

HAWTHORNE: But this thing the Professor let loose is evil! You said so yourself. And now you're trying to say that they've been helping mankind for a 100,000 years!

JO: Yes, and you say they come from another planet. Well then, what's all this jazz about witchcraft and covens and so on?

THE DOCTOR: But don't you see? All the magical traditions are just remnants of their advanced science. And that is what the Master is using.

HAWTHORNE: Then these creatures are linked with the Black Arts. They are evil.

THE DOCTOR: Amoral, perhaps. They help Earth, but on their own terms. It's a scientific experiment to them. Just another laboratory rat.

YATES: Then what's the Master up to?

THE DOCTOR: He's established a link with a Daemon. What worries me is the choice... domination by the Master or total annihilation!

JO: This... Daemon, could destroy the world?

THE DOCTOR: What does any scientist do with an experiment that fails? He chucks it in the rubbish bin.

JO: The end of the world!

25. THE VICARAGE.

(THE MASTER *is well into his speech, and such is his gift for persuasion that* THE VILLAGERS *are swept up in his oratory.*)

THE MASTER: Now as I told you, this is not going to be a sermon...

>*(There is a small laugh from the crowd.)*

... but all the same, I do beg of you to listen careful-ly, because this could be the most important day in your lives. Now as you know, I am a newcomer among you, and yet already I feel that I know you all. For instance you, Mr Thorpe... are you still padding the grocery bills of the local gentry?

>*(There is a gasp from the crowd.)*

THORPE: What are you on about? Th... Th... That's slander!

THE MASTER: Now, now, don't deny it, I know. And you Charlie... how's your conscience? Do you think you can man-age to balance the Post Office books in time? And you, Mr Grenville. Has your wife come back from her sis-ter's yet? Will she ever come back, do you suppose?

>(THE VILLAGERS *are bewildered, rather than annoyed, that all their innermost dark secrets seem to be known.)*

No, no, no, please. Please don't be angry with me. I assure you that I am on your side. Now listen. If you'll do what I say, you can all of you get what ever you want in this world. When you want it. If you listen to me!

26. THE CLOVEN HOOF PUB.

THE DOCTOR: Now, the Daemon will appear three times... and the third time he will probably tell us what our fate is to be. Now, he'll be in the cavern somewhere, awaiting the Master's second call.

BENTON: Then if we know where he is, why don't we go and find him?

THE DOCTOR:	You'd be wasting your time, Sergeant. At the moment he's so small, he's practically invisible.
JO:	But, Doctor...
THE DOCTOR:	Jo, would you get me a piece of paper and a pencil, please.

(She does so and he starts scribbling away, muttering to himself. BERT enters.)

BERT:	I wondered if you'd all care for a bite to eat?
BENTON:	Yes please.
JO:	No thanks, not just now. The Doctor's a bit busy.
BERT:	Oh, well er... is it all right if I get on with a bit of clearing up?
JO:	Yes, fine. If you could do it quietly.
BERT:	You won't know I'm here.
JO:	Thank you.

(He busies himself in the background. YATES' walkie-talkie beeps.)

YATES:	Greyhound Two. Come in please. Over.

27. UNIT MOBILE HQ.

BRIGADIER:	Is that you, Yates? Now look, we're going to blast our way in. I'm calling up the artillery and RAF strike command. You lot had better evacuate to the cellar. Over.

28. THE CLOVEN HOOF PUB.

THE DOCTOR:	Give me that!

(*He grabs the walkie-talkie from* CAPTAIN YATES.)

You'll do no such thing, Lethbridge-Stewart. Of all the idiotic suggestions! In the first place, the energy released would only strengthen the barrier. In the second place, it would provoke the most appalling reprisals. And in the third place, I've got a better idea. Over.

29. UNIT MOBILE HQ.

BRIGADIER: Well, what? I'm not going to sit here like a spare... like a spare lemon waiting for the squeezer. Do you hear me? Over.

30. THE CLOVEN HOOF PUB.

THE DOCTOR: Have you got the mobile HQ there?

BRIGADIER (*oov*): Yes, of course.

THE DOCTOR: With the new Mark Four-A condenser unit?

31. UNIT MOBILE HQ.

(THE BRIGADIER *looks over to* OSGOOD *who nods.*)

BRIGADIER: Apparently.

THE DOCTOR (*oov*): Good, then I've got your problem solved... and mine. We're going to build a diathermic energy exchanger. Is your technical fellow there?

(THE BRIGADIER *nods to* OSGOOD, *who comes over to the microphone.*)

BRIGADIER: He's listening.

32. THE CLOVEN HOOF PUB.

THE DOCTOR: Right. Well tell him to build an EHF wide band-width, variable phase oscillator, with a negative feedback circuit, tuneable to the frequency of an air molecule at er... what is the temperature up at the barrier, Brigadier?

33. UNIT MOBILE HQ.

(THE BRIGADIER *glances at* OSGOOD, *who shrugs helplessly.*)

BRIGADIER: We've no idea what you're talking about, Doctor. Over.

34. THE CLOVEN HOOF PUB.

THE DOCTOR: Well, it's a simple enough question. Over.

BRIGADIER (*oov*): No, what you said earlier. The oscillating feedback bit.

THE DOCTOR: All right. I'll come out and explain it to you myself. Yates and Benton can stay here and keep an eye open... only don't touch anything 'til I get there. Understood?

(BERT, *who has been listening in to all this, under the guise of tidying up, leaves the room, unnoticed.*)

BRIGADIER (*oov*): All right Doctor, we'll try it your way. But get a move on, will you?

THE DOCTOR: I'll be with you in ten minutes.

35. UNIT MOBILE HQ.

BRIGADIER: Make it five. Over and out.

36. THE CLOVEN HOOF PUB.

(THE DOCTOR *gives the walkie-talkie back to* CAPTAIN YATES.)

JO: Of all the idiotic plans! As if blowing things up solves anything.

THE DOCTOR: Jo, the Brigadier is doing his best to cope with an almost impossible situation. And since he is your superior officer, you might at least show him a little respect. Coming?

(*He sweeps out, with* JO, *looking rather hurt, following.*)

37. THE VICARAGE.

(THE MASTER *is still in full flow, his audience almost hypnotised.*)

THE MASTER: I ask you what you want in life... and I offer it to you. I tell you that everything is possible if you do as I say. Everything!

(*There is a murmur of approval from the audience, but suddenly* BERT *bursts in, effectively breaking the spell.*)

BERT: Mr Magister!

(THE MASTER *is furious at this interruption.*)

THE MASTER: Why do you interrupt me?

BERT: The Doctor is...

THE MASTER: Ssssh!

> (BERT *whispers in* THE MASTER'*s ear.* THE MASTER *nods and dismisses him.* BERT *exits.* THE MASTER *beckons* GIRTON, *who is in the crowd. He comes forward and* THE MASTER *whispers instructions to him.* GIRTON *leaves, but these interruptions have completely destroyed* THE MASTER'*s hold over the crowd.)*

WINSTANLEY: What's all this about obedience and submission? You said that we were going to rule.

> (THE MASTER *realises that he has lost control and snaps.)*

THE MASTER: You rule? Ha! Why, you're all less than dust beneath my feet.

WINSTANLEY: Preposterous!

THE MASTER: You choose to question me, do you? Very well, I will give you another choice. Obey me or I shall destroy you.

WINSTANLEY: Well, if that's your brave new world, you can keep it. I'm getting out of here, and if the rest of you've got any sense, you'll come with me.

> (WINSTANLEY *starts to walk away down the stairs.)*

THORPE: I reckon the Squire's right. Come on, let's get out of here.

> (THE MASTER *throws back his head and again there is a chattering sound. Almost at once the window flies open, and* BOK *leaps into the room. The audience gasps in fear as* THE MASTER *snaps*

his fingers and points at WINSTANLEY. BOK *points a claw at* WINSTANLEY *and he is instantly vaporised.)*

THE MASTER: Right. Is anybody else agreed with the Squire?

(Not surprisingly, nobody does.)

Thank you. It does my heart good to know I have such a willing band of followers.

(The villagers cower in complete terror.)

Now, today is May Day. Go and enjoy yourselves.

(They start to move.)

Celebrate the festival with your families. When I need you all I shall summon you again.

38. THE VILLAGE GREEN.

(The UNIT helicopter is standing in the middle of the green. GIRTON *approaches and gets in.)*

39. THE CLOVEN HOOF PUB.

*(*CAPTAIN YATES *is watching from the window. As soon as he sees what* GIRTON *is doing he rushes out.)*

40. THE VILLAGE GREEN.

*(*CAPTAIN YATES *hurls himself at* GIRTON, *now seated at the helicopter controls, and manages to pull him out onto the ground.* YATES *fights hard, but* GIRTON *is completely oblivious to the heavy blows that* YATES *deals him.* GIRTON *catches* YATES *a glancing blow to the side and leaps back into the*

cockpit. As he takes off, YATES *recovers and fires several shots at the fast receding helicopter. Realising he is too late, he desperately looks around, and seeing a motorbike parked nearby, makes a dash for that and drives off after the helicopter.)*

41. A COUNTRY ROAD.

(THE DOCTOR *and* JO *are driving along in Bessie.* THE DOCTOR *sees the helicopter coming towards them and brings Bessie to a halt.)*

JO: Look.

(The helicopter swoops down out of the sky and thunders directly overhead.)

THE DOCTOR: What's happening? I told Yates and Benton to stay in the pub.

(The helicopter banks steeply and turns, swooping down again, this time even closer to them.)

Who's flying that thing? That's not Benton!

JO: Well, it's certainly not Mike... look!

*(CAPTAIN YATES *is fast approaching on the motorbike.)*

Well, whoever it is, they're trying to kill us!

THE DOCTOR: Come on Jo... We're in for a bumpy ride.

*(THE DOCTOR *starts Bessie again and heads off down the road, but soon has to pull frantically off to one side to avoid a collision as the helicopter again swoops towards them.* YATES *pulls alongside them and shouts.)*

YATES: He's handling it like an expert.

THE DOCTOR: Like a man possessed, you mean. Look out, he's coming back.

YATES: I'll try and draw him off.

THE DOCTOR: No, you keep away. It's me he's after, not you.

(Again the helicopter swoops down.)

42. *Exterior UNIT Mobile HQ.*

(THE BRIGADIER, SERGEANT OSGOOD *and a number of UNIT troops are watching this, powerless to help.)*

BRIGADIER: What is Captain Yates up to? He'll kill the lot of them.

OSGOOD: No, sir. That's Captain Yates over there.

43. *Inside the Barrier.*

(YATES *tries again to shoot down the helicopter, but fails.* JO *looks up angrily at the helicopter, as it swoops down once more.)*

JO: What's he trying to do?

THE DOCTOR: Trying to drive us into the heat barrier!

(They turn once more, but the helicopter steadily pursues them, driving them ever closer to the blackened turf which marks the heat barrier. YATES *continues to shoot at the helicopter.)*

44. *Exterior UNIT Mobile HQ.*

BRIGADIER: Straight for the heat barrier. Get back. Back!

45. INSIDE THE BARRIER.

JO: The heat barrier. We're heading straight for it.

46. EXTERIOR UNIT MOBILE HQ.

BRIGADIER Back!
& OSGOOD:

47. INSIDE THE BARRIER.

THE DOCTOR: Hang tight, Jo. Hang on tight. Now!

(As they are about to enter the blackened area, THE DOCTOR *flings the steering wheel as hard as he can and Bessie screeches round, barely inches from certain destruction.* JO *is flung from the car and rolls across the ground. The helicopter, unable to turn in time, hits the barrier and explodes in a huge ball of flame.)*

48. THE CHURCHYARD.

(THE MASTER *looks up and sees a mushroom of smoke on the horizon. He goes back into the church, with a look of satisfaction on his face.)*

49. INSIDE THE BARRIER.

(THE DOCTOR *and* YATES *rush over to* JO, *who is lying unconscious on the ground.)*

YATES: How is she?

THE DOCTOR: She's had a nasty knock on the head. She'll be all right. We're going to load her into Bessie and get her down to the pub. She'll need rest and quiet.

YATES: Okay. What about you?

THE DOCTOR: I think I'd better have a word with the Brigadier. He's probably bursting a blood vessel by now.

> (THE DOCTOR *jumps onto the motorbike and roars off.* YATES *gently puts* JO *into Bessie.*)

> *50. THE CAVERN (EVENING).*

> (THE MASTER *enters wearing his cloak. He looks at the marked stone, then goes forward to prepare the ritual. The altar is now set.* BOK *follows him, like a monkey.*)

> *51. THE BARRIER.*

> (THE DOCTOR *roars up on the motorbike and dismounts, coming over to within a few feet of where* THE BRIGADIER *is standing, on the other side of the barrier.*)

BRIGADIER: £20,000 of UNIT money gone up in a puff of smoke!

THE DOCTOR: You've got the mind of an accountant, Lethbridge-Stewart. So, this is your heat barrier, is it?

BRIGADIER: Yes, and I advise you to keep your distance.

THE DOCTOR: Oh yes?

> (*He picks up a fairly large stone and tosses it towards* THE BRIGADIER. *It vaporises instantly, in a puff of smoke.*)

Hm... even rock!

BRIGADIER: Wood, rock, four inch armour plate; you name it, we've tried it. It's impenetrable.

THE DOCTOR:	A hasty and inaccurate assessment, Brigadier. Tell me, have you got enough cable to reach those high tension pylons over there?
BRIGADIER:	Should have. Why?
THE DOCTOR:	We'll need at least 10,000 volts to get through this lot.
BRIGADIER:	All right. I'll lay things on.
THE DOCTOR:	Good. Only, please hurry. We may have very little time left.
BRIGADIER:	Sergeant Osgood.
OSGOOD (*oov*):	Sir?
BRIGADIER:	Better come and listen to the Doctor. You've got to build the wretched thing.

(OSGOOD *runs up.*)

OSGOOD:	What's the principle, sir?
THE DOCTOR:	Negative diathermy, Sergeant. Buffer the molecular movement of the air with reverse phase shortwaves. It's quite simple.
OSGOOD:	Simple? It's impossible!
THE DOCTOR:	Yes, well, according to classical aerodynamics, it's impossible for a bumble-bee to fly!

52. THE CAVERN.

(THE MASTER *begins an incantation.*)

53. A BEDROOM AT THE CLOVEN HOOF PUB.

(JO *is lying in bed and seems to be delirious.* DOCTOR REEVES *is with her.*)

JO: Cavern! He said the danger was in the cavern!

(She struggles to get up.)

REEVES: Just lie still, my dear. Try to relax. This won't hurt.

(He administers an injection. She ignores him.)

JO: But the Doctor! I must help him find the Master!

YATES: Take it easy, Jo. As soon as he gets back, we'll all go and sort the Master out. Now, don't worry.

JO: But we must go now...

(She starts to fall back into unconsciousness.)

... there's no time...

(She trails off.)

REEVES: That's better. A few hours sleep and she'll be as right as rain.

54. THE CAVERN (NIGHT).

(THE MASTER'*s invocation is reaching a climax.*)

THE MASTER: Io Evohe... Io Evohe, Azal!

(His voice echoes round the cavern.)

I would speak with you. Show yourself!

(There is a rushing sound. The earth again starts to shake and THE MASTER *starts to look a little uncertain.)*

55. THE BARRIER.

(THE BRIGADIER *and* THE DOCTOR *are flung about*

as the ground begins to shake, violently.)

56. *A Bedroom at The Cloven Hoof Pub.*

(JO is awakened by the noise and the shaking. She sits up in bed, terrified.)

57. *The Cloven Hoof Pub.*

(MISS HAWTHORNE and BENTON are both clinging to the bar. YATES is thrown about the room and other objects crash to the floor.)

HAWTHORNE: The Demon! If he comes out, we shall all die!

58. *The Cavern.*

(THE MASTER is looking up in terror, as an enormous presence towers over him. He cowers away from it.)

THE MASTER: No. No, stop! Go back to the mark! Go back! You will destroy me! Stop! No! No!

EPISODE FOUR

1. THE CAVERN (EVENING).

(THE MASTER's invocation is reaching a climax.)

THE MASTER: Io Evohe... Io Evohe, Azal!

(His voice echoes round the cavern.)

I would speak with you. Show yourself!

(There is a rushing sound. The earth again starts to shake and THE MASTER starts to look a little uncertain.)

2. THE BARRIER.

(THE BRIGADIER and THE DOCTOR are flung about as the ground begins to shake, violently.)

3. A BEDROOM AT THE CLOVEN HOOF PUB.

(JO is awakened by the noise and the shaking. She sits up in bed, terrified.)

4. THE CLOVEN HOOF PUB.

(MISS HAWTHORNE and BENTON are both clinging to

>   *the bar.* YATES *is thrown about the room and
>   other objects crash to the floor.)*

HAWTHORNE: The Demon! If he comes out, we shall all die!

>   *5. THE CAVERN.*

>   (THE MASTER *is looking up in terror, as an enormous
>   presence towers over him. He cowers away from it.)*

THE MASTER: No. No, stop! Go back to the mark! Stop!

>   *6. THE BARRIER.*

THE DOCTOR: Look, get a move on with the heat exchanger. We've
                  got to get it charged and through this barrier and
                  down to the village before it's too late.

>   *(The machine is being loaded into a jeep by the
>   UNIT soldiers.)*

>   *7. THE CAVERN.*

THE MASTER: No, no! Back! Back!

>   (THE MASTER *picks up a tall, iron candle-holder
>   and thrusts it forward.)*

                  In the name of the Unspeakable One, back! Nathame,
                  Cinamade. Back!

>   *8. A BEDROOM AT THE CLOVEN HOOF PUB.*

>   (JO *looks around in bewilderment as memory
>   gradually recovers.)*

JO: Where am I?

(She suddenly remembers.)

The cavern. I must get to the cavern.

(She gets up and goes over to the door and opens it. From below she can hear voices.)

YATES (*oov*): Well, I'm going over there to see what's going on.

HAWTHORNE (*oov*): You can't, dear boy, the Doctor told us to stay here.

BENTON (*oov*): And we can't just leave Jo alone.

(JO quietly closes the door and goes over to the window. She opens it and climbs out.)

9. *EXTERIOR THE CLOVEN HOOF PUB.*

(JO climbs out of the bedroom window onto the flat roof. She sees a ladder left nearby and climbs down it to the ground.)

10. *THE CLOVEN HOOF PUB.*

YATES: I'm going to see what's happening.

HAWTHORNE: Oh, you can't. It's too dangerous.

BENTON: The Doctor told us to stop here, sir.

YATES: Oh, all right.

11. *THE BARRIER.*

(SERGEANT OSGOOD is busy working on the machine, while a group of UNIT soldiers are running a heavy cable over towards the pylons some distance away.)

THE DOCTOR:	No, man, no! You're trying to channel the entire output of the National Power Complex through one transistor! Reverse it.
OSGOOD:	Reverse what?
THE DOCTOR:	Reverse the polarity.
OSGOOD:	Look, we'd get along much faster if we knew what we were doing, sir.
THE DOCTOR:	Yes, I couldn't agree with you more, Sergeant. Now let's concentrate, shall we?

(THE BRIGADIER *hastily approaches*.)

BRIGADIER:	Right. I've fixed with Nuton for the power to be off for fifteen minutes. Ready to link up?
OSGOOD:	No, sir.
BRIGADIER:	Well when will you be ready for heaven's sake?
THE DOCTOR:	About next Christmas, I shouldn't wonder. At a rough estimate, of course.
OSGOOD:	Look, if you push 10,000 volts through this lash-up you'll blow it anyway.
BRIGADIER:	Just do as you're told, Sergeant. The Doctor knows what he is doing.

(OSGOOD *is not convinced*.)

OSGOOD:	Right, sir. Right Jenkins, have you got that junction box lined up?

(THE BRIGADIER *turns to* THE DOCTOR.)

BRIGADIER:	*Do* you know what you're doing?
THE DOCTOR:	My dear chap, I can't wait to find out!

(*He smiles*.)

12. THE CAVERN.

(The voice of AZAL *resonates throughout the cavern.)*

AZAL:	Speak!
THE MASTER:	I am the Master. I called you here.
AZAL:	That I know. Tell me why you now call me.
THE MASTER:	Give me your knowledge and your power.
AZAL:	Why?
THE MASTER:	So that I may rule these primitives on Earth here and help them to fulfil your plan.
AZAL:	You are not one of their kind.
THE MASTER:	No, I am superior to them. That's why I should be their leader.
AZAL:	There is another here of your race.
THE MASTER:	He has been destroyed.
AZAL:	No. He lives! I would speak with him.

(THE MASTER *is not very surprised. He knows how many times before* THE DOCTOR *has escaped from his death plots.)*

THE MASTER:	I think not.
AZAL:	Take care, creature. With your few pitiful grains of knowledge you have summoned me here. But I am not your slave... and you are not immortal!
THE MASTER:	Forgive me, Mighty One, forgive me. Nevertheless, I claim that which is rightfully mine.

AZAL:	Your mind is superior to mankind's, and your will is stronger.
THE MASTER:	Then I am to be your choice?
AZAL:	I shall consider. Now leave!
THE MASTER:	But you *will* come again?
AZAL:	I shall appear but once more. So be warned... there is danger. My race destroys its failures. Remember Atlantis!
THE MASTER:	Yes, but surely...
AZAL:	Be silent! I am the last of the Daemons. This planet smells to me of failure. It may be that I shall destroy it. You still wish me to come once more?
THE MASTER:	I do.
AZAL:	Very well. Now go!

(THE MASTER *bows and backs away. As* AZAL *begins to shrink again, a great ball of heat and light envelopes the church.*)

13. THE VESTRY.

(THE MASTER *tumbles out of the door that leads to the cavern and slams it shut. His face is triumphant.*)

14. THE CHURCHYARD.

(JO *is edging her way round the church when the effects of* AZAL'*s diminishment are felt. The ground shakes and* JO *clings to some ivy for sup-*

port. The ivy seems to wrap itself around JO, *as if trying to choke her.*)

15. *THE CLOVEN HOOF PUB.*

(CAPTAIN YATES, SERGEANT BENTON *and* MISS HAWTHORNE *are thrown to the floor.* YATES *struggles to get up, but the shaking is so severe that it is impossible.*)

16. *THE BARRIER.*

(THE DOCTOR *and* THE BRIGADIER *look towards the village. Although they are some distance away, the effects can still be felt.*)

THE DOCTOR: He's going. I must get back. The next time could be the finish. Sergeant Osgood, can you operate that machine now?

OSGOOD: Well, I'm not quite sure...

THE DOCTOR: Yes, well you'll have to. We may have very little time left.

(*He climbs onto the motorbike.*)

OSGOOD: Wait, Doctor! I still don't understand how you lock the pulse generator to the feedback circuit. They'll never be in phase.

THE DOCTOR: Well, of course they won't. That's the whole point!

OSGOOD: Well, how do you do it then?

THE DOCTOR: Oh dear, oh dear, oh dear! All right, I'll explain... once again. Only this time please listen!

17. THE CAVERN.

(The glow from the marked flagstone, the origin of AZAL's *manifestations, is slowly fading.)*

18. THE CLOVEN HOOF PUB.

(The shaking is dying down. YATES *manages to get to his feet and rushes upstairs.)*

YATES: Jo... Jo... Jo!

19. A BEDROOM AT THE CLOVEN HOOF PUB.

*(*YATES *bursts into the room.)*

YATES: Are you all right, Jo?

(He sees the empty bed and then the open window, and at once realises what has happened.)

Little idiot!

(He turns and runs out.)

20. THE CLOVEN HOOF PUB.

HAWTHORNE: Are you all right?

BENTON: More or less. What about you?

HAWTHORNE: Shaken, I'll admit.

*(*YATES *rushes downstairs.)*

YATES: Jo's gone. Out of the window. I'm going after her.

BENTON: Do you know where she is, sir?

YATES: I know all right. She'll have gone to the cavern.

HAWTHORNE: No!

BENTON: Trust her!

YATES: Look, when the Doc gets back, tell him what's happened.

BENTON: Be careful, sir. I don't want you to cop it like I did.

YATES: Not if I can help it.

(He leaves the pub.)

HAWTHORNE: Sergeant?

(She offers him a drink from behind the bar.)

BENTON: Thank you.

21 THE VESTRY.

(THE MASTER is busy giving instructions to BERT.)

THE MASTER: And make sure you do the job properly. The Doctor's been in my way for far too long.

BERT: Right.

THE MASTER: You know I was very foolish to speak with Azal alone. Next time I shall use the full ceremony. Every possible member of the coven must be present. If I am going to control Azal, I need every ounce of power I can summon up. Very well.

(He dismisses BERT.)

22. THE CHURCHYARD.

(YATES drops down behind a gravestone as he sees BERT coming out of the vestry. BERT gets into a car

and drives off. YATES *moves off again and does not see* JO, *nearby, fall unconscious out of the ivy.)*

23. *THE BARRIER.*

(THE DOCTOR *is just finishing his explanation, having drawn a complicated circuit diagram on the windshield of the motorbike.)*

THE DOCTOR: ... and it comes out here. Right?

OSGOOD: Right... I think.

THE DOCTOR: Good grief, man! It's as simple as Einstein's Special Theory of Relativity!

BRIGADIER: We'll manage, Doctor.

THE DOCTOR: Good. When you get that thing finished, bring it through the barrier and down to the village at once. All right?

(He roars off on the motorbike.)

BRIGADIER: You know, Sergeant, I sometimes wish I worked in a bank!

(Without waiting for a reply, he goes off to supervise some of his other men.)

Right! At the double there!

24. *THE CHURCHYARD.*

(JO *comes to her senses. She picks herself up and runs towards the vestry. She opens the door and enters.)*

25. *THE VESTRY.*

(JO *enters, goes across the room, and opens the door to the cavern.*)

26. *THE CAVERN.*

(JO *enters the cavern and cautiously moves forward. She suddenly catches sight of* BOK, *now stone again and apparently inanimate, in it's niche. She barely manages to stifle a scream. She recovers and moves forward again. As she turns to look behind her a hand is suddenly clamped over her mouth. Her agonised eyes swivel... and she sees that her captor is* MIKE YATES!)

YATES:	Ssssh!
JO:	Mike!
YATES:	They're in and out all the time. Why didn't you stay in bed?
JO:	I had to find out what was going on.
YATES:	You're an idiot. This place is alive with booby traps.
JO:	What?
YATES:	Spells, elementals... the Doctor's force-fields...

(JO *is petrified. She looks around the cavern.*)

JO:	Where? Where are they?
YATES:	All over. Here I'll show you. The book, there.
JO:	Yes?

(*He indicates to* JO *for her to hand him one of the books. She does so.*)

YATES: Now watch this.

(YATES *tosses the book onto the inscribed flag-stone. There is a rushing sound and the book is torn into a thousand pieces, all whirling around in the sudden wind.*)

JO: A horrible conjuring trick!

YATES: You think so? Remember Benton. Now come on, let's get out of here... ssssh!

(*They withdraw into an alcove as a hooded member of* THE COVEN *comes in and places something on the altar.* YATES *signals* JO *to keep quiet.*)

27. A COUNTRY LANE.

(THE DOCTOR *is riding along and, in spite of the urgency of the situation, is clearly enjoying riding the motorbike. Suddenly a bullet ricochets past his face and he swerves. From behind a nearby bush,* BERT *is firing at him. He fires two more shots and* THE DOCTOR *deliberately steers the motorbike off the road and up a grassy hill, aiming for the cover of the woods at the top. Just before he reaches them, a lucky shot hits one of the tyres and he is thrown from the motorbike. He is immediately on his feet and running.* BERT *fires again, but misses.* THE DOCTOR *escapes into the woods, with* BERT *in hot pursuit.*)

28. THE CAVERN.

(JO *and* YATES *are still in hiding. Another member of* THE COVEN *enters and busies himself at the*

*altar, preparing for a sacrifice. He places a large
knife at the centre.* JO *and* YATES *whisper to each
other.)*

JO: Mike, I'm scared.

YATES: Don't worry. The Doc'll be here soon; Benton
knows we're here.

29. THE CLOVEN HOOF PUB.

(BENTON is speaking into his walkie-talkie.)

BENTON: Hello, Greyhound. This is Trap Three. Do you read
me? Over?

(The only sound he hears is static.)

Hello, Greyhound. Greyhound. Do you read me?
Over.

(Again there is nothing but static. MISS
HAWTHORNE *comes in with a tray.)*

HAWTHORNE: I've brought you a nice cuppa, Sergeant. I hope you
like China?

BENTON: Oh for Pete's sake, Miss Hawthorne!

HAWTHORNE: What's the matter, don't you like tea?

BENTON: Something's gone badly wrong. We've no idea
what's happening to Miss Grant and the Captain.
The Doctor should be back here by now. I can't get
through to the Brigadier and... you're nattering on
about tea!

HAWTHORNE: You must learn the art of waiting, Sergeant. The
Doctor will come... or else he won't... and that's all
that can be said. Now... milk or lemon?

(BENTON *returns to the radio.*)

BENTON: Hello, Greyhound, Greyhound. Do you read me? Over.

30. THE BARRIER.

BRIGADIER: Sergeant!

OSGOOD: Sir?

BRIGADIER: Is it you making that horrible racket? I can't get a thing through. The air's thick with it.

OSGOOD: Yes sir, he's... testing you see, sir. This is fascinating! It's not right yet, but even on the battery it's pumping it out. It's a sort of controlled resonance principle, you see..

BRIGADIER: Yes, well never mind the mumbo-jumbo. Keep the wretched thing switched off 'til it's ready.

OSGOOD: I'm sorry, sir, can't. I must finish the tests.

BRIGADIER: Well, how long are you going to be?

OSGOOD: Matter of minutes, sir. I've got the hang of it now!

(*He returns to the machine. Moments later it explodes.* OSGOOD *looks up, his face covered with soot.*)

Half an hour, sir. At least!

31. THE VICARAGE.

(*Someone is banging on the front door.* THE MASTER *comes down the stairs and goes over to open it.* BERT *rushes in.*)

BERT: Magister... I'm sorry.

THE MASTER: The Doctor got away.

BERT: How could you know that? Well... yes he did. You see what happened...

THE MASTER: Excuses waste time. Where is he?

BERT: I lost him in the woods. I expect he's making his way back to the village by now.

THE MASTER: Then we must see that he is given a suitable welcome, mustn't we.

32. UNIT MOBILE HQ.

BRIGADIER: What's the matter with you, Benton? I want to speak to the Doctor. Over.

33. THE CLOVEN HOOF PUB.

BENTON: But I... But I thought he was still with you, sir. Over.

34. UNIT MOBILE HQ.

BRIGADIER: No, he left here... oh, a good forty minutes ago.

35. THE CLOVEN HOOF PUB.

BRIGADIER (*oov*): Hasn't he turned up yet?

BENTON: Well no, sir. Not a sign of him. Do you suppose he's all right, sir? Over.

BRIGADIER (*oov*): Piled up that wretched motorbike!

BENTON: Do you want me to go and look for him, sir? Over.

36. *UNIT MOBILE HQ*.

BRIGADIER: No. Better give him a bit longer. But if he does turn up, will you tell him that we're running into a bit of trouble with our... feedback phasing... is that right, Osgood?

OSGOOD: Yes.

BRIGADIER: Yes, that's it, Benton. Tell him that, will you? Over and out.

37. *THE CLOVEN HOOF PUB*.

(BENTON *turns off the walkie-talkie.*)

BENTON: That's it, then.

HAWTHORNE: More waiting, Sergeant.

BENTON: Yes, the Captain and Miss Grant should have been back ages ago... the Doctor seems to have disappeared completely. Look, I'm going to go and have a nose around out there.

HAWTHORNE: You stay where you are. I'll go and look for them.

BENTON: Sorry ma'am. Will you *please* do as you're told.

(*He insists she sit down and then he goes over to the window.*)

HAWTHORNE: Anyone in sight?

BENTON: Just a few villagers. Will you tell the Doctor I've gone to the cavern.

HAWTHORNE: Wait! Listen...

(*The unexpected and incongruous sound of morris dancers, with their music, their jingling bells and wooden clacking beating out a rhythm, can be heard approaching the village green.* BENTON *and* MISS HAWTHORNE *gaze out of the window in astonishment.)*

BENTON: What do they think they're doing?

38. *THE VILLAGE GREEN.*

(A procession of morris dancers, led by BERT, *approaches. Some, like* BERT, *dressed as the Paperman, are in traditional costume, but many villagers in everyday clothes also join in. The dancers gather round a maypole in the centre of the village green.)*

39. *THE CLOVEN HOOF PUB.*

HAWTHORNE: Charming!

BENTON: They're round the twist, if you ask me.

HAWTHORNE: It's May Day. We always have the morris dancers on May Day. It's traditional.

BENTON: Hey, look! There's the Doctor.

40. *THE VILLAGE GREEN.*

(As THE DOCTOR *approaches the pub, the dancers, led by* BERT, *gradually surround him. At first he manages to weave amongst them, but gradually they tighten around him and start to lightly beat him with their ceremonial sticks.)*

THE DOCTOR: Yes, yes, most amusing... Now please let me pass. Any other time I'd gladly join you...

(The dancers start to hit THE DOCTOR *harder and harder, and as they surround him he is forced towards the maypole. All the while the music of the morris dancers continues. The mood quickly turns from celebration to ugliness and, as* THE DOCTOR *is pushed violently to the ground,* BERT *pulls out a gun from beneath his costume.)*

What on earth is going on? What are you doing? What on earth is this?

BERT: You're being invited to join our May Day revels, Doctor. I'm sure you don't want to disappoint us... or Mr Magister.

41. *THE CLOVEN HOOF PUB.*

HAWTHORNE: They seem to have stopped.

BENTON: Yeah... Hey, what's happening? Well that doesn't look very traditional.

42. *THE VILLAGE GREEN.*

*(*THE DOCTOR *is dragged along by* THE VILLAGERS *and tied to the maypole.)*

43. *THE CLOVEN HOOF PUB.*

BENTON: Look, I've got to go and help.

*(*BENTON *makes for the door.)*

HAWTHORNE: You can't, there are too many of them.

*(*BENTON *ignores her. He takes out his gun and heads for the door. As he opens it, he is met by*

one of the villagers armed with a stave. The man crashes the stave down on BENTON's *wrist, knocking the gun to the floor. The two fight, with* BENTON *seeming to get the worst of it.* MISS HAWTHORNE *looks helplessly around, then picks up her bag and hits the villager with it on his head. He immediately falls unconscious to the floor. She helps* BENTON *to his feet.)*

Did he hurt you?

BENTON: What happened?

HAWTHORNE: I hit him with my reticule.

(She opens the bag and produces a crystal ball.)

On these occasions the outcome's a certainty.

BENTON: Very handy. Thank you.

HAWTHORNE: I always carry it with me.

*(*BENTON *goes to pick up his gun.)*

No Sergeant, wait! Look, I know these people. They're not wicked... most of them anyway.

BENTON: So?

HAWTHORNE: So, it's up to us to explain to them how mistaken they are. Now listen carefully...

44. The Village Green.

*(*THE VILLAGERS *dance round* THE DOCTOR, *securing him ever more tightly with the maypole ribbons.* THE DOCTOR's *hands are obscured from view by his cloak.)*

THE DOCTOR: The Master is planning to make slaves of you all. I am the only one who has a chance of stopping him.

BERT: He's lying. He is the enemy. Mr Magister will care for you... give you everything you've ever wanted.

THE DOCTOR: That's nonsense! All the Master will bring upon you is disaster.

BERT: He is the enemy. He's a black witch! Witch! Do you hear... witch!

(The villagers are startled by this accusation and the music stops.)

And you've always known what you must do with a witch, haven't you? Thou shalt not suffer a witch to live!

THE DOCTOR: Are you out of your mind?

BERT: Shut up! That's right, friends, Thou shalt not suffer a witch to live. Burn him!

THORPE: Burn him!

VILLAGERS: Burn him! Burn him!

45. THE CAVERN.

(THE MASTER throws some powder onto the thurible and there is a flash of fire and smoke.)

THE MASTER: Io Evohe.

COVEN: Io Evohe.

(YATES and JO are watching the ceremony from their hiding place.)

THE MASTER: As my will so mote it be.

COVEN: Nema.

THE MASTER: Harken to my voice, oh dark one; ancient and awful. Supreme in artifice; bearer of power. Be present here at my command, and truly do my will. Eva, Evara, Egabala, Gad, Gadoal, Galdina! As my will so mote it be.

COVEN: As thy will so mote it be!

> *(In the niche where he has been crouching, immobile,* BOK's *eyes light up.)*

> *46. THE VILLAGE GREEN.*

> *(THE DOCTOR's feet are now buried in a pile of straw and kindling.* THORPE *puts a match to a wooden torch and approaches the maypole. As he does,* MISS HAWTHORNE *strides across the green.)*

BERT: Now!

> *(THORPE moves towards* THE DOCTOR.*)*

HAWTHORNE: Stop! You will bring a terrible retribution upon yourselves if you persist.

BERT: Shut up you silly old fool.

HAWTHORNE: You would dare to harm the great wizard, Quiquaequod?

THORPE: Wizard?

HAWTHORNE: You wouldn't listen to me before... and now you are in the power of the Magister. You know I speak the truth.

BERT: Get on with it, man.

HAWTHORNE: No, wait! Listen to me. Under the Magister, you have been frightened, injured, your property destroyed. Serve the great Quiquaequod! In him lies peace and great joy!

BERT: If he's such a great magician, let's see him untie himself.

THE DOCTOR: You choose to mock the great Quiquaequod? Well I will not.

BERT: Because you can't!

(He snatches the torch from THORPE *and starts towards* THE DOCTOR.*)*

HAWTHORNE: Give him a sign of your power, O mighty one.

*(*THE DOCTOR *realises that* MISS HAWTHORNE *is up to something, but can't quite figure out what.)*

THE DOCTOR: What had you in mind?

HAWTHORNE: I know! That lamp. Shatter it.

THE DOCTOR: Shatter it? Yes, yes, of course.

(She nods encouragement at him. He looks puzzled, but goes along with it.)

THE DOCTOR: Lamp. I order you to shatter!

(The lamp immediately shatters. THE VILLAGERS *are amazed. Even* BERT *is taken aback.* THE DOCTOR *realises at once what is happening and starts to enjoy himself.)*

You see? That could have been you. Now, all of you. Look at the er... weathercock on the church tower?

(He looks at MISS HAWTHORNE, *who nods.)*

47. *THE CLOVEN HOOF PUB.*

(*From the window of the pub, on the other side of the green,* BENTON *aims his gun.*)

48. *THE VILLAGE GREEN.*

THE DOCTOR
(*oov*):
Weathercock... now!

(*The weathercock spins violently around.* THE VILLAGERS *exclaim excitedly.*)

VILLAGERS:
He must be a magician. He is a magician.

HAWTHORNE:
Bert, drop that torch! You're beaten and you know it!

BERT:
Am I?

(BERT, *although equally amazed, is not prepared to give up so easily, and lifts the torch into the air.*)

49. *THE CLOVEN HOOF PUB.*

(BENTON *fires again from the pub and the torch is sent flying, out of his hand.* BERT *gives a sharp cry.* THE VILLAGERS, *however, are now convinced.*)

50. *THE VILLAGE GREEN.*

THE DOCTOR:
Thank you. Daughter of Light, would you kindly untie my bonds?

(MISS HAWTHORNE *smiles and steps forwards, but before she can untie* THE DOCTOR, BERT *pulls out his gun.*)

BERT: You don't scare me with a lot of daft tricks. Mr
                   Magister has the real power.

HAWTHORNE: His power is worth nothing in comparison.

BERT: Right! Let's see if you can turn aside a bullet.

                   (He points his gun directly at THE DOCTOR.*)*

                   51. THE CLOVEN HOOF PUB.

                   (BENTON'*s line of sight is blocked by the crowd.
                   He is unable to help* THE DOCTOR.*)*

                   52. THE VILLAGE GREEN.

THE DOCTOR: I'll give you one more chance. Look behind you.

BERT: That's the oldest trick in the book.

THE DOCTOR: Very well, let my familiar spirit bring that car to me.

                   *(He looks over at Bessie, parked nearby and, as
                   he does so, he fumbles in the pockets beneath his
                   cloak. Bessie's engine starts up and she trundles
                   slowly towards the maypole.* THE VILLAGERS *start
                   to murmur.* BERT *refuses to look round, and keeps
                   his gun aimed at* THE DOCTOR.*)*

BERT: You won't frighten me, you know. Think I'm as stu-
                   pid as this lot?

                   (Bessie comes up behind BERT *and he turns round
                   at the last moment, just in time to be knocked off
                   his feet by the car.* MISS HAWTHORNE *runs over to*
                   THE DOCTOR *and starts to untie him.)*

HAWTHORNE: You really *are* a magician!

THE DOCTOR: I'm sorry to disappoint you, madam, but if I were, I'd hardly need your assistance in extricating myself from this... this sacrificial gift-wrapping!

(SERGEANT BENTON *comes running up.*)

BENTON: How on earth did you do that, Doctor?

THE DOCTOR: Elemental, my dear Benton.

(BERT *suddenly decided to run for it.* BENTON *leaps after him, and floors him with a rugby tackle.*)

BENTON: Oh no you don't chap. We've all got a date with the Master, haven't we?

53. *THE CAVERN.*

THE MASTER: Wons Saet Ihw Sawece Elfstib Malelt Tilad Ahyram!

(*A member of* THE COVEN *produces a feebly flapping chicken.*)

COVEN: Io Evohe.

THE MASTER: Azal! We have power over life, you and I. Accept this life, I now dedicate to thee. Athame Malelt Tilad Ahyram!

(*He raises the ceremonial knife.* JO *cannot bear it any longer and rushes out into the cavern. She wrestles with* THE MASTER, *desperate to prevent him from sacrificing the chicken.*)

JO: No! Stop it! It's evil, can't you see that; it's evil!

THE MASTER: You're too late, my dear.

(*He raises his arms high.*)

Eko, Eko, Azal!

COVEN: Eko, Eko, Azal!

(At once the wind, the cold, the earth tremors and the noise all start up again. The face of THE MASTER *is triumphant as* AZAL *appears, growing rapidly in size until he towers above them.)*

THE MASTER: Azal! Ha, ha, ha, ha, ha, ha!

*(*THE MASTER*'s demonic laughter echoes round the cavern as* JO, YATES *and* THE COVEN *look in horror as they stare up at the face of... the Devil!)*

EPISODE FIVE

1. The Cavern (Day).

THE MASTER: Azal! We have power over life, you and I. Accept this life, I now dedicate to thee. Athame Malelt Tilad Ahyram!

(He raises the ceremonial knife. JO cannot bear it any longer and rushes out into the cavern. She wrestles with THE MASTER, desperate to prevent him from sacrificing the chicken.)

JO: No! Stop it! It's evil, can't you see that; it's evil!

THE MASTER: You're too late, my dear.

(He raises his arms high.)

Eko, Eko, Azal!

COVEN: Eko, Eko, Azàl!

(At once the wind, the cold, the earth tremors and the noise all start up again. The face of THE MASTER is triumphant as AZAL appears, growing rapidly in size until he towers above them.)

THE MASTER: Azal! Ha, ha, ha, ha, ha, ha!

(THE MASTER's demonic laughter echoes round the

cavern as JO, YATES *and* THE COVEN *look in horror as they stare up at the face of... the Devil!)*

2. THE BARRIER.

BRIGADIER: The last appearance... that's what the Doctor said.

OSGOOD: I'm working as fast as I can.

BRIGADIER: Well, it doesn't seem to be fast enough. You have five minutes, Sergeant!

(He turns to the rest of his men.)

Right. On our way in five minutes.

3. THE VILLAGE GREEN.

(The quaking, the wind and the noise are now subsiding. THE DOCTOR *and the others pick themselves up.)*

HAWTHORNE: The third appearance.

BENTON: In the cavern.

THE DOCTOR: Where else?

BENTON: We'd better get over there, hadn't we?

THE DOCTOR: Wait! All of you.

BERT: You see! This chap's frightened!

THE DOCTOR: Well of course I am frightened... so should you be... and your friend, Mr Magister.

4. THE CAVERN.

THE MASTER: Azal! Welcome.

(JO *makes a sudden dash to get away.*)

Bok! Stop them!

(CAPTAIN YATES *lifts his gun and fires. The bullets hit* BOK, *but ricochet off the stone of his body.* BOK *snarls and raises his hand as* YATES *fires again. A bolt of fire leaps from* BOK's *hand and the gun flies from* YATES' *hand, who realises the futility of his actions and gives up.*)

You are very wise, Captain.

(*Members of* THE COVEN *seize* JO *and* YATES.)

Prepare the girl in the ceremonial tabard. She will make a welcome addition to the Sabbat.

JO: No! No! Let me go. Mike help me, please! Let me go!

(YATES *tries to break free, but is knocked unconscious with the butt of his own gun.* THE COVEN *members leave, dragging* YATES *and a struggling* JO *with them.*)

5. THE VESTRY.

(YATES *is thrown down on the floor and his hands are tied behind his back.*)

6. THE VILLAGE GREEN.

THE DOCTOR: And we're facing the greatest danger the world has ever known! Now look, I've got to tell you the truth.

HAWTHORNE: Doctor, no!

THE DOCTOR: I've got to risk it.

THORPE: What are you talking about?

THE DOCTOR: I'm not a magician or a wizard or anything of the sort.

BERT: You see! I told you!

THE DOCTOR: But neither is the Master. I tricked you, yes, but only to save you from him.

BERT: To save your own life, you mean.

THE DOCTOR: Yes, of course, that too.

BERT: Well... there you are, do you hear, the lot of you? He admits it!

THORPE: Just pipe down for two minutes, Bert.

BERT: But you heard him.

THORPE: Shut up. We want to hear what he's got to say.

HAWTHORNE: But your car? How did you make it move by itself?

THE DOCTOR: Science... not sorcery, Miss Hawthorne. Look.

(He takes out the remote control unit and operates it. Bessie beeps her horn and flashes her headlamps.)

BENTON: Well, I'll be blowed!

THE DOCTOR: Your Mr Magister uses no more magic than that.

BERT: You're talking rubbish! The Master's a magician, I tell you!

THE DOCTOR: All his feats are based on science... either ours or the secret science of the Daemons.

BERT: Well, there you are! That proves you're talking nonsense. How could he have called him up in the first place except by sorcery?

THE DOCTOR: Well, he uses violent emotions - fear, hatred, greed.

THORPE: How?

THE DOCTOR: Well, the emotions of a group of ordinary human beings generate a tremendous charge of psycho-kinetic energy. This the Master channels for his own purpose.

HAWTHORNE: But that is magic. That's precisely what Black Magic is!

THE DOCTOR: No, Miss Hawthorne, I'm afraid not.

HAWTHORNE: Are you trying to tell me that the invocations, the rituals, even the Sabbat itself, are just so much window dressing?

THE DOCTOR: No, no, no, of course not. No, they are essential to generate and control the psionic forces... and to control the Daemon himself.

BENTON: Shouldn't we get over there and sort this Daemon thing out?

THE DOCTOR: How?

BENTON: Well, I could get the men...

THE DOCTOR: Yes?

BENTON: Well, we could...

THE DOCTOR: Exactly! All we can do is wait.

BENTON: What for?

THE DOCTOR: The energy-exchanger... this machine that the Brigadier is building for me. With that, I should be able to drain off our visitor's energy. Then perhaps we can 'sort him out'.

7. THE CAVERN.

THE MASTER: Azal! The time for decision draws near. Once more, I demand the power...

AZAL: You demand?

THE MASTER: Yes, and why not? Who in the whole galaxy is not my inferior? There is not one creature!

AZAL: Not... even... one?

(THE MASTER *realises that he is treading on dangerous ground.*)

THE MASTER: Not one... save the last of the Daemons!

(JO *is brought struggling into the cavern by two of* THE COVEN *members. She is now dressed in a long ceremonial robe.*)

Azal, accept this offering as a token of our fealty. As my will, so mote it be.

COVEN: As thy will, so mote it be.

THE MASTER: Io Evohe. Azal!

COVEN: Io Evohe!

(THE MASTER *snaps his fingers and* JO *is dragged forward.*)

Io Evohe! Io Evohe!

8. THE VESTRY.

(YATES *regains consciousness and struggles to his feet. He goes over to the door leading to the cavern and can hear the ceremony going on below. Desperately trying to free his hands, he goes over to the door leading outside. With a struggle, he manages to open it with his bound hands and stumbles out of the door.)*

9. *THE VILLAGE GREEN.*

(YATES *comes running across the green.)*

YATES: Doctor, Doctor!

(BENTON, *who has been holding* BERT, *hands him over to two of the villagers and runs to help* YATES.)

BENTON: Hold him!

YATES: Doctor, Doctor, it's Jo!

THE DOCTOR: Jo? I thought she was still in the pub?

YATES: They've got her in the cavern!

THE DOCTOR: What!

YATES: That creature's in there! The Master calls him Azal.

HAWTHORNE: Azal! Of course, Azael the fallen angel!

THE DOCTOR: Walkie-talkie.

(BENTON *hands his to* THE DOCTOR.)

Hello, Brigadier. Are you there?

10. *THE BARRIER.*

BRIGADIER: That you, Doctor? Over.

11. *THE VILLAGE GREEN.*

THE DOCTOR: Look, they've got Jo. That machine must come through now. Now, do you understand? Now!

12. *THE BARRIER.*

BRIGADIER: We're on our way, Doctor.

13. *THE VILLAGE GREEN.*

THE DOCTOR: Good, and put a watch up on that barrow will you... just in case the Daemon's ship reactivates.

14. *THE BARRIER.*

BRIGADIER: Will do, Doctor. Over and out.

(*He turns to* OSGOOD.)

You heard him, Sergeant. Now!

OSGOOD: I need...

BRIGADIER: That's an order, Sergeant. Now!

(OSGOOD *shrugs, pulls a switch and the machine starts to hum.*)

15. *THE VILLAGE GREEN.*

(THE DOCTOR *looks impatiently towards the direction in which* THE BRIGADIER *should be coming.*)

THE DOCTOR: Come on, Brigadier, get a move on.

16. *THE CAVERN.*

(JO *is still struggling and screaming as* THE MASTER *continues his preparations.*)

THE MASTER: I'm sorry, Miss Grant. But you are to be sacrificed in a noble cause.

JO: No! No!

          17. The Barrier.

          (In the background troops are climbing into jeeps.
          THE BRIGADIER *and* OSGOOD *anxiously watch the*
          heat-exchanger as wisps of smoke start to rise up
          from it.)

OSGOOD: It'll never take it, I tell you.

BRIGADIER: It must. Keep trying.

          18. The Village Green.

THE DOCTOR: Right, now some of you that way, but... but spread
          out. The rest of you, follow me.

          19. The Cavern.

          (A lookout at the top of the stairs shouts a warn-
          ing.)

LOOKOUT: Mr Magister. They're coming! They're coming!

JO: Doctor!

          *(*THE MASTER *snaps his fingers and* BOK *leaves the*
          cavern.)

          20. Exterior the Church.

          (The villagers recoil in terror as BOK *appears.*
          BERT *struggles, but is held by two men.)*

YATES: Right, Benton. You keep us covered, we'll get in at
          the back.

THE DOCTOR:	No! We must wait for the Brigadier!
YATES:	But what about Jo?
THE DOCTOR:	We won't help her by committing suicide.

(At this moment BERT *manages to break free. He runs towards the church.)*

BERT:	Magister! Magister!

*(*BOK *raises his hand.* BERT *sees what he is doing and screams a desperate plea.)*

No! No! Friend. I'm a friend!

(The words die on his lips, as there is a flash from BOK, *and* BERT *is instantly vaporised.)*

THE DOCTOR:	You see?

*(*THE DOCTOR *speaks into the walkie-talkie.)*

What's going on, Brigadier? You must hurry!

21. *THE BARRIER.*

BRIGADIER:	We're up to the maximum now, Doctor, and it's still no good.
THE DOCTOR (*oov*):	You'll have to use the booster.
OSGOOD:	If you do, sir, she'll blow us all sky high.
BRIGADIER:	We're coming through, Doctor. Over and out. Booster on.
OSGOOD:	But, sir!
BRIGADIER:	Damn it, man. Get on with it!

(THE BRIGADIER *pushes* OSGOOD *aside and oper-ates the booster himself. The noise from the machine rises even higher.*)

22. *THE CAVERN.*

(THE MASTER *holds the sacrificial knife high in the air, as he continues his dedication.*)

THE MASTER: O mighty Azal, in the name of Athame, I dedicate this offering.

JONES: No! No, Magister. It's not right!

(THE MASTER'*s eyes flash.*)

THE MASTER: To do my will shall be the whole of the law.

COVEN: To do thy will shall be the whole of the law.

JONES: It's not right, I tell you!

THE MASTER: Obey me!

23. *THE BARRIER.*

BRIGADIER: Look! It's working!

(*Smoke is pouring out of the machine, but a sort of tunnel has appeared through the barrier, with its edges marked by a strange, shimmering distor-tion.* THE BRIGADIER *goes towards it and tentative-ly reaches out with the end of his baton. It smoul-ders, but does not burst into flame.*)

All right, it's still hot, but passable. Right, start up... and keep to the tunnel.

(THE BRIGADIER'*s car drives through, followed by the first of the UNIT vehicles.*)

24. The Cavern.

(THE MASTER *is still facing a revolt by a few members of* THE COVEN, *who do not have the stomach for a human sacrifice.*)

THE MASTER: Obey me!

(*Suddenly* AZAL *roars as if in pain.* THE MASTER *looks up, and sees* AZAL *staggering and clutching his head.*)

25. Exterior the Church.

(THE DOCTOR *is shouting into the walkie-talkie.*)

THE DOCTOR: Look, what's going on, Brigadier?

BRIGADIER (*oov*): We're through, Doctor. Over.

THE DOCTOR: What, all of you?

BRIGADIER (*oov*): Yes, but not the machine.

THE DOCTOR: Well that should have come through first!

BENTON: Doctor, look!

(*He points to* BOK, *who is staggering around.*)

THE DOCTOR: The exchanger's working. It's bleeding off the energy.

26. The Barrier.

(OSGOOD *is busy disconnecting the power cables from the machine.*)

BRIGADIER: Come on, man. Bring it through. Get a move on.

OSGOOD: Sir. Right, Jenkins.

(The driver accelerates and races the jeep through the tunnel. The machine is smoking furiously and it emits an ominous shriek.)

BRIGADIER: Stop worrying, Doctor. We're through.

THE DOCTOR (*oov*): About time, too! Now get it over here, fast!

OSGOOD: Sir. Sir! I can't stop it. It's running away.

BRIGADIER: Osgood! Out of it. Get down, all of you!

(They all dive for cover, except OSGOOD *who stays with the machine, desperately trying to turn it off.)*

Osgood! Get down man!

(At the last moment, OSGOOD *jumps clear, just as the heat-exchanger blows up. As the sound of the explosion echoes away, there is dead silence.)*

27. *EXTERIOR THE CHURCH.*

THE DOCTOR: Brigadier? Brigadier! Are you all right?

BRIGADIER (*oov*): The machine's gone west. Blown itself up. Be with you right away. Over and out.

THE DOCTOR: A fat lot of good that'll do! Right, keep the others back, Captain Yates. I'm going in, before that creature recovers.

YATES: I'll come with you, Doctor.

THE DOCTOR: Alone!

THORPE: You can't go in now, sir. You said yourself, it'll be suicide.

> (THE DOCTOR *runs towards the church, dodging past* BOK, *who is starting to recover.*)

YATES: Doctor... wait!

> (*As* THE DOCTOR *reaches the vestry door,* BOK *raises his hand to fire.* THE DOCTOR *dives inside.*)

28. *THE VESTRY.*

> (THE DOCTOR *slams the door shut, and as he does so there is a loud explosion on the other side of the door.* THE DOCTOR *hurries over to the door leading to the cavern and opens it.*)

29. *THE CAVERN.*

THE MASTER (*oov*): Ah, Doctor. I've been expecting you.

> (THE DOCTOR *ignores* THE MASTER, *but is overwhelmed by the size of* AZAL, *who has fully recovered and is staring hard at* THE DOCTOR.)

You've saved me a lot of trouble by coming here. I am most grateful.

THE DOCTOR: Hello, Jo. I cannot tell you how glad I am to see you.

THE MASTER: How very touching.

30. *EXTERIOR THE CHURCH.*

> (THE BRIGADIER'*s car pulls up and he gets out.*)

BRIGADIER: Where's the Doctor?

YATES: Gone in there, sir.

BRIGADIER: Then what are we waiting for? Let's get after him.

YATES: Wait, sir. Look.

> (*He points at* BOK, *whose head is swinging malevolently from side to side, searching for his next victim.*)

BRIGADIER: What the blazes is that? Some kind of ornament?

YATES: Not exactly, sir. Watch.

> (YATES *picks up a rock and throws it towards* BOK, *who instantly raises his hand and vaporises it.*)

BRIGADIER: Yes, I see what you mean. Never mind, we'll soon fix him. Jenkins?

JENKINS (*oov*): Sir?

> (JENKINS *runs up carrying an assault rifle.*)

BRIGADIER: Chap with wings there. Five rounds rapid!

> (JENKINS *fires, but with no effect, the bullets ricochetting harmlessly off* BOK. THE BRIGADIER *and* YATES *look at each other, helplessly.*)

31. THE CAVERN.

THE MASTER: You realise, of course, that you're a doomed man, Doctor?

THE DOCTOR: Oh, I'm a dead man. I knew that as I came through that door. So you'd better watch out. You see, I have nothing to lose, have I?

THE MASTER: Enough!

> (*He turns to* AZAL.)

Azal... destroy him!

AZAL:	Who is this?
THE MASTER:	My enemy and yours, Azal. Destroy him.
AZAL:	This is the one we spoke of. He too is not of this planet.
THE MASTER:	He is a meddler and a fool!
AZAL:	He is not a fool... yet he has done a foolish thing, coming here. Why did you come?
THE DOCTOR:	I came to talk to you.
AZAL:	Talk then.
THE DOCTOR:	Certainly, but first let her go.
	(He indicates JO.*)*
THE MASTER:	No!
	(AZAL *raises his arm. There is a crackle of fire and* JO's *guards fall back with cries of pain.* JO *runs over to* THE DOCTOR.*)*
JO:	Doctor!
THE DOCTOR:	Are you all right, Jo?
JO:	I am.
AZAL:	You wish to talk?
THE DOCTOR:	Yes, I want you to leave this planet, while you still can.
AZAL:	You are bold!
THE DOCTOR:	Why not? I've got a machine outside that could annihilate you.
AZAL:	You lie.

THE DOCTOR: You've already felt its power.

AZAL: It is destroyed.

THE DOCTOR: One of them, yes. Not both.

AZAL: You lie! There was but one.

JO: Doctor!

AZAL: You have a regard for truth. Why do you lie?

THE DOCTOR: To try and make you listen to me.

AZAL: Why should I? I see no consequence of value.

THE MASTER: Then kill him! Kill him now!

AZAL: Very well.

> *(He lifts an arm, ready to strike.)*

JO: No!

THE DOCTOR: If you kill me now, you will wonder throughout eternity whether you should have listened to my words.

> *(AZAL does not drop his arm.)*

32. THE CHURCHYARD.

> *(UNIT soldiers are still firing at BOK, but to no avail.)*

YATES: Might as well use a peashooter on four-inch armour. Sergeant, get the bazooka set up... over there.

BENTON: Right, sir.

> *(He turns to JENKINS.)*

You... with me.

33. The Cavern.

(AZAL *has not moved.*)

THE MASTER: Well?

(AZAL *still does not move.*)

You waste time. I order you to kill him, Azal.

AZAL: I command. I do not obey.

(He drops his arm.)

THE MASTER: But I... I called you here, and you came.

AZAL: I answered your call because the time was come for my awakening. The time has come for the completion of the experiment... or its destruction.

THE MASTER: Then fulfil your mission by granting the ultimate power to me. Who else is there strong enough to give these humans the leadership they need?

THE DOCTOR: I seem to remember somebody else speaking like that... what was the bounder's name? Hitler... yes that's right, Adolf Hitler... or was it Genghis Khan?

THE MASTER: Azal, I have the will. You, yourself, said so.

AZAL: I am still not convinced.

THE DOCTOR: I'm very pleased to hear it.

AZAL: You wish to see this planet destroyed?

THE DOCTOR: By no means. You see, I have an alternative.

AZAL: State it.

THE DOCTOR: Leave humanity alone. Just go. You've done enough harm.

AZAL: We gave knowledge to Man.

THE DOCTOR: You certainly did. Thanks to you Man can now blow up the world; and he probably will. He can poison the water and the very air he breathes; he's already started. He can...

AZAL: Enough! Is Man such a failure then? Shall I destroy him?

THE MASTER: No! A strong leader can force him to learn!

AZAL: You are right. I have decided. I shall pass on my power.

THE MASTER: O mighty Azal, I thank you.

AZAL: But not to you... to him!

               (AZAL *points at* THE DOCTOR.)

JO: Doctor!

THE DOCTOR: No! No! I don't want it!

               34. THE CHURCHYARD.

               (The UNIT soldiers are still firing at BOK *with no effect.* BOK *points a hand at one of the soldiers and instantly vaporises him. The bazooka is set up.* YATES *gives the order.)*

YATES: Fire.

               (BENTON *fires, the bazooka spouts flame and the projectile scores a direct hit.* BOK *shatters into a thousand pieces.)*

BRIGADIER: Well done, Sergeant.

BENTON: Just a minute, sir. Look!

(As they stare in disbelief, the shattered remains of BOK *seem to jump back together again and* BOK *stands there once more, unharmed.)*

35. THE CAVERN.

AZAL: You refuse my gift?

THE DOCTOR: Of course I do. Don't you understand? I want you to leave. I want you to go away and give Man a chance to grow up.

AZAL: I cannot. My instructions are precise. I bequeath my power or I destroy all.

THE MASTER: Then you will give your power to me?

(THE MASTER can hardly believe his good fortune.)

AZAL: I shall. Time is short.

THE MASTER: What about him?

AZAL: He is not rational. He is disruptive. He must be eliminated.

(AZAL raises his arm and points it at THE DOCTOR. *Fingers of lightning leap from his hand and* THE DOCTOR *sinks to his knees in agony.)*

JO: No!

(Oblivious to the danger, JO *rushes in front of* THE DOCTOR, *shielding him from* AZAL's *deadly touch.)*

No! He is a good man. Kill me, not him!

(JO shuts her eyes, awaiting certain death. Nothing happens. She opens her eyes again, to see AZAL *swaying as if in pain. He is bathed in an orange glow and smoke pours from him.)*

AZAL: Aaargh! This action does not relate. There is no datum. It does not relate! Go! Leave me. All of you.

(A maelstrom erupts in the cavern and the ground beneath begins to shake, this time more violently than ever.)

36. THE CHURCHYARD.

(BOK suddenly turns back into inanimate stone. The shaking is apparent out here too, and the wind again begins to rise.)

BRIGADIER: Cease firing!

(THE BRIGADIER goes over to BOK and taps him on the head with his baton. He is just a harmless, stone gargoyle once more. The doors of the church burst open and THE DOCTOR and JO, followed by THE MASTER and the members of THE COVEN, pour out into the churchyard. As THE DOCTOR comes out he shouts a warning to THE BRIGADIER.)

THE DOCTOR: Run for it, Brigadier!

(Moments later there is an almighty explosion and the church explodes in a huge ball of flame.)

37. THE VILLAGE GREEN.

(As the echo from the explosion dies away, people peer out to see what has happened to the church. There is little left of it. BENTON points his gun at THE MASTER.)

BENTON: Get up. Don't try anything.

BRIGADIER: What happened in there, Doctor?

THE DOCTOR:	Well... by a ridiculous and foolhardy act of self-sacrifice, Jo here has managed to save us.
JO:	I did?
THE DOCTOR:	You did. You see Azal couldn't face a fact as irrational and illogical as her being prepared to give up her life for me. Look Jo, why don't you go and get out of that ridiculous garb?
JO:	Okay.
YATES:	So what happened?
THE DOCTOR:	Well, all his power was turned against himself. You might say he blew a fuse.

(From a long way away, in the direction of the barrow, comes a huge explosion.)

YATES:	Greyhound Two. Come in please. Over.
CHALMERS (*oov*):	Chalmers here at the dig, sir. Are you all right? Over.
YATES:	Couldn't be better. What's happening?
CHALMERS (*oov*):	Big bang at the dig, sir.
THE DOCTOR:	The spaceship. Automatic self-destruct, I suppose.
CHALMERS (*oov*):	And the barrier's cleared itself. Over.
YATES:	Good show. We're coming out now... with one prisoner. Over and out.
BRIGADIER:	Benton, get ready to move out.
BENTON:	Yes, sir. Right, you lot, you heard the man. The picnic's over.

(The UNIT troops prepare to leave. Without warning, THE MASTER *throws his ceremonial cloak over* BENTON'*s head, jumps into Bessie parked nearby and starts to drive away.* THE BRIGADIER *and* BENTON *at once open fire.)*

THE DOCTOR: Stop firing. You'll damage Bessie!

BRIGADIER: You want him to get away?

THE DOCTOR: Don't worry. Bessie will bring him back.

(Bessie obediently swings around and brings THE MASTER *back, straight into the muzzles of the UNIT guns. Realising that for the moment he is defeated, he raises his hands in surrender.)*

BRIGADIER: How on earth did you do that?

THE DOCTOR: Simple... If you know how.

*(*THE DOCTOR *laughs.* THE BRIGADIER *turns to* BEN-TON, *who quickly stops grinning and starts issuing orders.)*

BRIGADIER: Right, Benton, get 'em moved out. And take him with you. Maximum security guard.

BENTON: Yes, sir. Right. Get moving!

THE DOCTOR: And look after him. I want to deal with him later.

THE MASTER: Do you, Doctor? You always were an optimist, weren't you?

THE DOCTOR: Thank you for the compliment.

BENTON: All right. Move!

*(*THE MASTER *is loaded into the back of a jeep, surrounded by UNIT solders. As the jeep is driven off,* THE VILLAGERS *jeer and hiss at him.)*

HAWTHORNE: Listen!

THE DOCTOR: To what?

JO: Yes, the birds are singing again!

HAWTHORNE: And smell the flowers.

THE DOCTOR: Yes, well it makes a change from the smell of sulphur, doesn't it?

HAWTHORNE: The May Day miracle has happened again. The Earth is born anew.

(BENTON *comes up and reports to* THE BRIGADIER.)

BENTON: All under way, sir.

(The music of the May Day morris dancers starts up again.)

HAWTHORNE: Sergeant, we must do the fertility dance to celebrate.

BENTON: Oh no, I'm sorry ma'am. I'm still rather busy.

HAWTHORNE: Oh, nonsense Sergeant! Come along.

(She drags him off to the maypole, where the dancers are reforming to begin again.)

JO: Come on, Doctor.

(She too drags him off to the maypole, where they join in the dancing and celebration.)

YATES: Fancy a dance, Brigadier?

BRIGADIER: It's kind of you, Captain Yates... I think I'd rather have a pint.

(He looks over at The Cloven Hoof pub.)

THE DOCTOR: You're right, Jo. There is magic in the world after all!

(As they continue to dance, the peace and tranquility of a typical English village has once again returned to Devil's End.)

THE TRIBE OF GUM
Anthony Coburn
Edited by John McElroy

THE DAEMONS
Robert Sloman and Barry Letts
Edited by John McElroy

THE MASTERS OF LUXOR

THE TOMB OF THE CYBERMEN

For a complete list of Titan's Doctor Who publications,
please send a large stamped SAE to Titan Books Mail Order,
19 Valentine Place, London SE1 8QH.
Please quote reference DW6.